Masculinity of M

A Young Man's Handbook on Noble Masculinity

Masculinity of Muhammad ﷺ: A Young Man's Handbook
on Noble Masculinity

© 2023, Azhaan Mohammed

ISBN: 9798858526483

This book is designed to provide information on the
subject matter covered. It is sold with the understanding
that the author is not engaged in rendering professional
services. If professional advice or other expert
assistance is required, the services of a competent
professional should be sought.

About The Authors

In the world of literature and mentorship, Hafiz Azhaan Mohammed and Hafiz Taha Ansari serve as a beacon of inspiration. Azhaan's writings have consistently resonated with readers, and his newest offering, *Masculinity of Muhammad ﷺ: A Young Man's Handbook on Noble Masculinity,* reinforces this legacy. It marks the third significant milestone in his literary journey, with his preceding work, *Character of Muhammad: Peace Be Upon Him,* having left an indelible mark on many.

But Azhaan's influence extends well beyond books. He has advocated youth development through various initiatives, keenly understanding the power of mentorship in molding the leaders of tomorrow. Alongside these, Azhaan and Taha have made significant contributions to political campaigns in their history together. Azhaan was entrusted with key roles in coordinating and guiding volunteers for political canvassing in his appointed area, playing a pivotal role in the outreach and strategic efforts of the campaign. Through these experiences, Azhaan's ideology emerged clearer: to live life aspiring to greatness while seeking to uplift those around him. This commitment to societal betterment extends to Azhaan's philanthropic endeavors, such as leading water well projects in underserved regions, highlighting a comprehensive approach to community engagement.

Balancing his academic commitments as a college student, Azhaan has always believed in the virtues of discipline and perseverance. These qualities are evident in his pursuit of martial arts. Holding a black belt in Tae-Kwon-Do, he integrates the principles of this discipline into his daily life and teachings, emphasizing the importance of focus, dedication, and resilience. It's this fusion of physical discipline and mental rigor that sets him apart in his mentorship approach.

Sacred Haqq, founded by Azhaan, is a testament to his visionary approach to mentorship. Beyond just guiding, it's about empowering young writers to narrate their stories, fostering a new generation of thinkers and writers. The collaboration with Hafiz Taha Ansari on this book wasn't merely a co-authored work; it was the embodiment of Sacred Haqq's mission.

Hafiz Taha, with his understanding of masculinity, brought a rich tapestry of insights to this partnership. Serving in the Singaporean Armed Forces, Taha showcased a blend of dedication to both his faith and his nation.

The roots of Azhaan and Taha's partnership date back to their high school days. Their leadership roles in their respective Muslim Students' Associations fostered a bond rooted in shared values and vision. During their time as leaders, Azhaan and Taha worked to build relationships between not only their respective high school MSA's, but also a network of other MSA's. Over the years, their collaborations evolved, from initiating youth programs to taking center stage as speakers at public events. And now, taking their collaborations to the next level, they publish this book, *Masculinity of Muhammad ﷺ A Young Man's Handbook on Noble Masculinity,* hoping to further impact and inspire the hearts of many.

Islamic Review and Validation by Hafiz Ikhlas Ansari, Ph.D.

Hafiz Ikhlas Ansari is as a distinguished authority in Islamic education and scholarship. Having penned multiple writings, he is not just an author, but a beacon of knowledge in the field. His foundational education from *Madrasah Al-Arabia Tajweedul Qur'an* paved the way for his academic journey. Subsequently, he secured two master's degrees — one emphasizing Islamic Studies from *Karachi University,* and the other focusing on the modern disciplines of Information Systems and Computer Science from the *National University of Singapore.*

For over two decades, Dr. Ansari has been imparting wisdom to his students, teaching them the tenets of Islamic studies. His classrooms have been spaces where traditional knowledge meets contemporary insights, creating an enriching learning experience for his students.

Going beyond his academic achievements, Dr. Ansari has also been an active advocate for peace, harmony, and understanding. He has actively participated in and led initiatives aimed at dispelling misconceptions about Islam. His passion for community service is evident through his involvement in *Light Upon Light,* an organization he founded in Chicago to further these ideals. His guidance also extends to his local community in Chicago where he is the Imam of his mosque and directs the Hifzh department. His consultancy work at the *IQRA International Educational Foundation* also served as a testament to his commitment to Islamic education at various levels.

However, Dr. Ansari's influence isn't just localized; it's global. He serves on the board of directors for organizations such the *North American Imam's Federation* and the *World Council of Muslims for Interfaith Relations.* And on an international level, he is recognized for his contributions as a member of the board of governors for the *Z International School* in Karachi, Pakistan, and an advisor for the *Society of Educational Research in Lahore.* He is also the religious advisor and group leader for *Chicago Hajj and Umrah.*

This book has been privileged to be reviewed by Dr. Ansari, assuring readers of its adherence to the profound teachings and values of Islam.

Masculinity of Muhammad ﷺ

A Young Man's Handbook on Noble Masculinity

Contents

Directory of Phrases Used

Allah	God's name.
Quran	Muslims' holy book revealed to Prophet Muhammad ﷺ by Allah through His angel Gabriel.
Masjid	Also known as mosques, places of worship for Muslims.
Muhammad	The name of Allah's final Prophet who, by the Will of Allah, spread the message of Islam.
ﷺ	Transliteration is "Salallahu Alayhi Wa Salam."

	Translates to "Peace be upon him." This phrase most commonly follows the Prophet Muhammad's name. For example, one could say: • Prophet Muhammad ﷺ was an amazing man. • Muhammad ﷺ was an amazing man. • He ﷺ was an amazing man.
عليه السلام	Transliteration is "Alayhis-Salaam." Translates to "Peace be upon him."

	This phrase most commonly follows the names of Prophets other than Prophet Muhammad ﷺ. Although, it can be said after the name of Prophet Muhammad ﷺ as well. For example, one could say: • Prophet Isa عليه السلام was an amazing man. • Musa عليه السلام was an amazing man. • Ibrahim عليه السلام was an amazing man.
Hadith	Recorded teachings and sayings of Prophet Muhammad ﷺ.

| Rasulullah | Translates to "Prophet or Messenger of Allah."

We use it as a reference to Muhammad ﷺ.

An example of how *Rasulullah* ﷺ can be used is:
- Rasulullah ﷺ was the greatest man to walk the earth. |
|---|---|
| Quran | The holy book of Islam containing the Words of Allah that He revealed to Prophet Muhammad ﷺ. |
| Sunnah | The habits or actions that our Prophet ﷺ performed that aren't necessarily mentioned in the Quran. |

	A few examples are: • The way he ﷺ slept. • His daily routine ﷺ. • The way he ﷺ cut his nails. • The way he ﷺ used to walk.
Sahaba	Muslim companions of the Prophet ﷺ.
رضي الله عنه	Transliteration: "Radi Allahu Anhu" (used when referring to the males). Translates to "God be pleased with him." This phrase is most commonly used following the sahabas' names.

	For example, one could say: • Anas bin Malik رضي الله عنه was an amazing man.
رضي الله عنها	Transliteration: "Radi Allahu Anha" (used when referring to the females). Translates to "God be pleased with her." This phrase is most commonly used following the sahabas' names. For example, one could say: • Aisha رضي الله عنها was an amazing woman.

Alhamdulillah	Translates to "All praise be to Allah."
	We use this phrase when thanking Allah.
	Examples of how the phrase *Alhamdulillah* could be used are:
	- Alhamdulillah for this food.
	- Alhamdulillah for everything I have.
	Allah says in the Quran:
	وَإِذْ تَأَذَّنَ رَبُّكُمْ لَئِن شَكَرْتُمْ لَأَزِيدَنَّكُمْ وَلَئِن كَفَرْتُمْ إِنَّ عَذَابِي لَشَدِيدٌ ﴿٧﴾
	And [remember] when your Lord proclaimed, "If you are grateful, I will surely increase you [in

	favor]; but if you deny, indeed, My punishment is severe." (Quran 14:7)
InSha'Allah	Translates to "If Allah Wills." We use this phrase when planning for something, or when we hope for something to happen. Examples of how the phrase *InSha'Allah* could be used are: • InSha'Allah we'll go to the movies tomorrow. • InSha'Allah I will finish writing this book soon. Allah says in the Quran:

	وَلَا تَقُولَنَّ لِشَيْءٍ إِنِّي فَاعِلٌ ذَلِكَ غَدًا ﴿٢٣﴾ إِلَّا أَن يَشَاء اللَّهُ وَاذْكُر رَّبَّكَ إِذَا نَسِيتَ وَقُلْ عَسَى أَن يَهْدِيَنِ رَبِّي لِأَقْرَبَ مِنْ هَذَا رَشَدًا ﴿٢٤﴾ *And never say of anything, "Indeed, I will do that tomorrow," except [when adding], "If Allah Wills." And remember your Lord when you forget [it] and say, "Perhaps my Lord will guide me to what is nearer than this to right conduct."* (Quran 18:23-24)
Imaan	Faith in Islam which encompasses believing in six main articles: <ul><li>Belief in Allah.</li><li>Belief in Angels.</li><li>Belief in the Holy Books.</li></ul>

	- Belief in the Prophets. - Belief in the Day of Judgement. - Belief in Divine Destiny (Qadr).
Wudu	The Islamic purification ritual for cleansing parts of your body. It is considered an ablution where you must wash your face, hands, arms, and feet.
Dhikr	Remembrance of Allah by verbally saying phrases in His remembrance. A few examples are: - Subhanallah (Glory be to Allah). - Alhamdulillah (Praise be to Allah).

	• Allahu Akbar (Allah is the Greatest). • Astaghfirullah (I seek the Forgiveness of Allah).
Deen	Translates to Religion • My deen is Islam.
Caliph	Refers to the leader of the Muslim Ummah.
Shahada	The Declaration of Faith.
Adhan	The first call to prayer. • Serves as an announcement that a prayer time has begun.
Iqamah	The second call to prayer, recited right before the actual prayer begins.

	• Serves as a signal that the congregation is about to start the prayer.

Masculinity of Muhammad

A Young Man's Handbook on Noble Masculinity

In the footsteps of Muhammad ﷺ we tread,
A guide for all, in heart and head.
His masculinity, a shining light,
A beacon for us, day and night.

Through his strength and wisdom, we see,
The epitome of masculinity.
His compassion and kindness, a true measure,
Of the balance in strength we should treasure.

In the example of Muhammad ﷺ we find,
A man who was the strength of a kind.
A leader who stood for what is right,
Guiding his people, day and night.

May we follow in his path ﷺ,
And emulate his masculinity, unswerving and
steadfast.
For in doing so, we honor his name,
And find true honor and fame.

In the masculinity of Muhammad ﷺ, we see,
The ultimate example of true masculinity.
May we strive to embody his ways,
And find true honor and grace in our days.

Introduction

In a world shrouded with the darkness of injustice, chaos, arrogance, and wickedness, came a man — a beacon of hope to herald a new era. He came into a world where the burial of daughters prevailed, the relentless conflict between the Persian and Byzantine empires transgressed, and the strong preyed on the weak. In this age, when slavery was common, abuse of the poor was the norm, and ancestry dictated societal presence, he came as a light who would alter the course of humanity forever.

He came to the most backward, ignorant people of the time — the most oppressed economically, politically unstable, and impulsive people: the people of Arabia. To them, he came with Allah's message of Islam, extinguishing the ignorance in their hearts through the teachings of mercy and love. He taught humanity that no man is greater than the other in terms of worldly affairs and that every son of Adam is created equal.

Throughout his life, he preached justice, equality, mercy, and understanding. He despised the idea of racism and stated: *"All mankind is from Adam and Eve. An Arab has no superiority over a non-Arab, nor a non-Arab has any superiority over an Arab; also a white has no superiority over black, nor a black has any superiority over white except by piety and good action."*[1] This was Muhammad Rasulullah ﷺ — the man who would redefine the term, *masculinity.*

In the Name of Allah, the Most Merciful, the Most Compassionate. All praise be to Him, the Lord of the worlds, the One who brings His will into existence by simply stating, *Be,* and it is. May the Peace and Blessings of Allah be upon our beloved role model, Muhammad Rasulullah, upon his loved ones, upon

---

[1] Musnad Ahmad 22978

his companions, and upon all those who follow him ﷺ till the Day of Judgment — the Day of Resurrection.

Only those who have delved into the depths of his character ﷺ, possessing both accomplishment and an open mind, can truly grasp an understanding of the natural influence and genuine respect that he ﷺ possessed — the character that attracted love — the character that was set as a model for all of humanity to follow.

Conversely, in contemplating the character of Rasulullah ﷺ, it is only natural to ponder whether there are aspects of his character ﷺ that hold specific lessons for men. Are there elements within his noble persona ﷺ that illuminate the path to true masculinity? Can his character ﷺ serve as a guiding light for men striving to reach their full potential? To uncover the answers to these questions, this book, *Masculinity of Muhammad ﷺ: A Young Man's Handbook on Noble Masculinity,* highlights the commendable and blessed manhood that the Prophet ﷺ possessed. In this book, you will uncover the ways he ﷺ led those around him to success ﷺ. You will find how his noble masculinity ﷺ served him ﷺ in attaining dignity, honor, and respect in society. And you will learn about the bridge between his methods of success ﷺ and the physical, psychological, scientific, societal, and spiritual benefits taught by contemporary research.

Then, through the pages of this book, you will unravel the wisdom underlying Rasulullah's laws of masculinity ﷺ. And by drawing connections between his teachings ﷺ and contemporary research, will you gain insights into the methods that you, as a young man, must incorporate into your life. Only by doing so will you find yourself building an honorable and respectable reputation in the eyes of society, and, more importantly, in the Eyes of Allah.

Prophetic Productivity

Exploring the life of our Rasool ﷺ, we uncover a profound realization. While he ﷺ embodied the qualities of a spiritual leader, his teachings ﷺ did not shy away from the principles of worldly success. As a man, you will find that to truly excel in life, you must first gain mastery over the factors that influence your existence. You must master your thoughts, time, and routine before anything else. Why?

Because as a man, it is your primary responsibility to support and provide. However, how will you hope to display a positive demeanor to the world, if there is nothing backing it? How will you be able to challenge the world and grow if you cannot even control your own desires — your own nafs?

But what is *nafs*? The nafs is a wild beast, incessantly growling and yearning to overpower you. It represents your innermost desires, your shortcomings in personal growth, and your tendencies toward laziness. In Arabic, *nafs* literally translates to *self.* And the greatest battles you will often face will be against yourself. Thus, by winning these battles on a daily basis, can you grow and make an impact on the world around you. Only then, after taming your nafs, can you embark on your transformative journey toward embracing and embodying true masculinity.

In this chapter, *Prophetic Productivity,* you will learn the universal ideologies in Islam that directly contribute to and measure your inward success. While you may find some of these laws of productivity aligning with your preexisting understanding of Islam, it's crucial that you are able to fully comprehend them. You may know that consistency is key, but do you know the psychology behind it? Or you may understand that making dua can open doors for you, but have you read 21st-century research on it? Setting the theme for this book, this chapter will bridge the gap between prophetic practices and contemporary research on productivity.

Persistence

In the ever-shifting sands of your life, time stands as an unwavering force, beckoning you forward with every ticking second. You may find yourself contemplating the famous quote, *'Everyone has the same 24 hours.'* Though these words are frequently heard, their proper application may elude you.

Take a look at the journey of Elon Musk, whose unwavering dedication drives him to work tirelessly, seemingly around the clock. He recognizes the value of every minute, embracing a 24/7 mindset as he strives towards his goals.

Meanwhile, you may find yourself squandering away those same hours, indulging in meaningless activities that offer little to no good in terms of personal growth.

So to start fixing yourself, take a moment to reflect upon your daily schedule. Are there pockets of time when you could redirect your focus toward endeavors aligning with your aspirations? Are there moments in your day spent in idle distraction that could instead be channeled toward meaningful pursuits? Remember, it is within your control to shape the narrative of your life and make each day count.

❖ Understand: While you work towards your dreams, remember to also maintain balance in your deen. Because only by balancing your work and worship of Allah can you be successful. Allah says in the Quran:

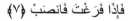

فَإِذَا فَرَغْتَ فَانصَبْ ﴿٧﴾

25

So once you have fulfilled [your duty], strive [in devotion],

(Quran 94:7)

وَإِلَى رَبِّكَ فَارْغَبْ ﴿٨﴾

turning to your Lord [alone] with hope.

(Quran 94:8)

Although, you may not know how to be productive in your life. So how can we blame you for your lack of productivity when the root problem has yet to be identified? But to reach the base of the problem, you must first ask yourself what time management truly means. Where are you lacking behind, and what methods can you apply to manage your time better, according to the sunnah of Rasulullah ﷺ?

This subchapter, *Persistence,* will teach you just that. Not only will you learn the prophetic keys to time management, but you will also learn the scientific and psychological studies conducted on them to lead a more fruitful, prophetically influenced life.

Early Productivity

Dhuhr, the prayer that provides a much-needed break between work, followed by Asr, the salat that holds immense significance, as neglecting it is akin to losing one's family and possessions.[2] Then comes Maghrib, the salat that prepares you for the night, and finally, Isha, the key to a blissful sleep. Unfortunately, it's a sad reality that this is the prayer schedule many Muslims follow, excluding the day's first salat: Fajr.

While many sleep past Fajr, those who seek its blessings discover the key to true productivity. Because in order for you to grasp the essence of time management, we must first delve into the

---

[2] Sahih al-Bukhari 552 - Book 9, Hadith 29

power of Fajr and go above and beyond what is strictly obligatory. Starting off, this includes embracing the two rak'ah sunnah that precede the obligatory Fajr prayer. Rasulullah ﷺ said, *"The two Rak'ah before the dawn (Fajr) prayer are better than this world and all it contains."*[3]

Then, after concluding the two obligatory rak'ah of Fajr, stay seated for as long as you are able to and complete your morning dhikr. The Prophet ﷺ said, *"The angels keep on asking Allah's forgiveness for anyone of you, as long as he is at his Musalla (praying place) and he does not pass wind (Hadath). They say, 'O Allah! Forgive him, O Allah! be Merciful to him."*[4]

Here, consider both the prayer and the Remembrance of Allah after your prayer, acts of mindful meditation. And considering that Fajr salat is

---

[3] Riyad as-Salihin 1102 - Book 8, Hadith 112
[4] Sahih al-Bukhari 445 - Book 8, Hadith 94

prayed before sunrise, let's look at what contemporary science says about this practice.

Science Behind Early Meditation:

According to the American Psychological Association, meditation first thing in the morning can lead to a more positive outlook on your day. They say, *"Starting your day with a morning meditation can help you begin your day with less grogginess, more gratitude, and with the right mindset for a more productive and satisfactory day."*[5]

They then state that this meditation practice could bring about significant health benefits regardless of whether you're a morning person or a night owl. Now you may think, *'Well, that's great and all, but how can this help me with time management?'* When you begin your days early in the worship of Allah, there are health benefits, but

---

[5] Sejal Shah: The Art of Living

more than that, the answer lies in the statement! You are starting your days earlier than the masses!

Assume the world wakes up around 9 AM on weekends/holidays, yet you are awake from 6, sometimes 5 AM. You've now given yourself an extra three to four hours a day. Now, you can use these early hours to either amplify your spirituality, or improve your worldly life. Either spend them improving your closeness to Allah, or pay them in worldly self-improvement. But, regardless of how you want to spend your time, do not go back to bed after waking up. Because Rasulullah ﷺ asked Allah to bless those mornings so they may serve as a time of productivity for us, an advantage the sahaba utilized well.

Sakhr al-Ghamidi رضي الله عنه narrated that the Prophet ﷺ said, *"O Allah, bless my people in their early mornings.' When he sent out a detachment or an army, he sent them at the beginning of the day. Sakhr was a merchant, and he would send off his merchandise at the beginning of the day; and he became rich and had much wealth."[6]*

Consistency

Now that you've prophetically begun your day and gifted yourself with a few extra hours, what comes next? The next step is establishing a schedule and maintaining consistency in your endeavors. The Prophet ﷺ said, *"Take up good deeds only as much as you are able, for the best deeds are those done regularly even if they are few"[7]* Conversely, understand that consistency does not mean overwhelming yourself excessively every day. Instead, stick to deeds that you know are accomplishable and practice them on a daily basis. Allah says in the Quran:

---

[6] Sunan Abi Dawud 2606 - Book 15, Hadith 130
[7] Sunan Ibn Majah 4240

إِنَّهُ لاَ يُحِبُّ الْمُسْرِفِينَ ﴿٣١﴾

Indeed, He likes not those who commit excess.
(Quran 7:31)

Thus, it is crucial to understand that big goals can only be accomplished through small steps accumulating over time. Perhaps you're a new writer struggling to write. Instead of writing for hours on end per day, limit yourself to an hour a day. Or perhaps even a page a day. Then, as your writing skills get better, start increasing your workload. All you need to do is stick to your work daily instead of overburdening and burning yourself out.

James Clear, author of *Atomic Habits,* states, *"All big things come from small beginnings. The seed of every habit is a single, tiny decision. But as that decision is repeated, a habit sprouts and grows stronger. Roots entrench themselves and branches grow. The task of breaking a bad habit is like uprooting a powerful oak within us. And the task of building a good habit is like cultivating a delicate flower one day at a time.*[8]

❖ Understand: In Islam, you will find a plethora of deeds and actions that can please Allah. You find deeds such as fasting, also known as the deed that expiates sins, or Tahajjud, the prayer of the prophets, and many other important acts of worship. They hold great significance, yet also require much effort. So now consider the status of those deeds that are done consistently when the Prophet ﷺ said that the best actions to Allah are the ones that are done consistently.

However, just because consistency means engaging in actions that you can be consistent with, doesn't mean you don't push yourself. As a man, work to gradually increase your tolerance, just like you

---

[8] James Clear: Atomic Habits

would increase your weight at your gym during workouts.

Although, going back to the main point, it's still crucial to not overburden yourself, especially when it comes to worship. Your body is entrusted to you by Allah, and it has a right over you, so do not hurt it. Strive towards your goals, but do so in a moderate fashion. If you are able to pray for an hour at night without hurting yourself, then pray it. But don't aim for that right off the bat, potentially ruining your health trying to please Allah, because the Prophet ﷺ advised against it.

The Prophet ﷺ once saw a man engaging in excessive worship, so he ﷺ instructed him to avoid doing so. Abdullah bin Amr bin Al-As narrated, *"Allah's Messenger ﷺ said, 'O Abdullah! Have I not been formed that you fast all the day and stand in prayer all night?' I said, 'Yes, O Allah's Messenger ﷺ!' He said, 'Do not do that! Observe the fast sometimes and also leave them (the fast) at other times; stand up for the prayer at night and also sleep at night. Your body has a right over you, your eyes have a right over you and your wife has a right over you.'"*[9]

Science Behind Consistency:

Whether immersed in a school project, embarking on an entrepreneurial journey, or working to integrate a new spiritual practice into your life, remember that consistency is the key to success. In psychology, according to Klaus Grawe, consistency can often be described as the *"compatibility of many simultaneously transpiring mental processes."*[10]

Or in other words, when someone's actions are consistent, it causes a multitude of mental

---

[9] Sahih al-Bukhari 5199 - Book 67, Hadith 133. Note: When the Prophet ﷺ is speaking about fasting and prayer in this situation, he ﷺ is not talking about the mandatory fasts of Ramadan nor the mandatory five daily salats. Rather he ﷺ is referring to voluntary fasts outside of Ramadan and voluntary salats apart from the five daily. Allah knows best.

[10] Grawe: Consistency Theory 2007, P.170

processes in the mind to work together in a compatible and cohesive manner. This may lead to a sense of clarity and purpose in your thoughts and actions. Yes — your thoughts also, because those thoughts, your unconscious mind, can manifest your reality. According to *The Science of Psychotherapy*, *"Consistency regulation is predominantly unconscious and only rises to conscious awareness during exceptional circumstances… Grawe considers consistency to be a core principle of mental functioning."*[11]

Now with consistency, you'll find overlaps with the power of affirmation. This concept essentially states that you are what you think you are! Or rather, what you say you are. But what exactly are affirmations? Think of affirmations as powerful tools when teaching yourself a new skill or working toward changing your mindset. They hold the ability to

---

[11] SoP: Consistency Theory

transform your worldly views, self-views, and even beliefs — all through the act of repetition. By consciously repeating positive statements to yourself, you can gradually shift your outlook toward a more optimistic and empowering perspective.

For instance, say you're sleepy, yet find yourself buried in tons of studying for an exam tomorrow. It's only 9 PM, yet you feel yourself dazing off. Instead of complaining about your sluggishness, tell yourself how energized you are. Stand in front of a mirror, and keep saying to yourself, *'I'm not tired; I can keep going. I'm not tired; I can keep going. I'm not tired; I can keep going.'* Same deal when you find yourself nervous, scared, or insecure. Stand nourishing your mind, your nafs with positive self-talk.

Researchers conducted a study examining the impact of affirmations on the brain. They found, through neuroimaging, that when you engage in self-affirmation exercises, specific regions of your brain associated with positive thinking and future-oriented planning exhibit heightened activity.

According to Christopher Cascio and his team of researchers, *"neural activity went on to predict changes in sedentary behavior consistent with successful affirmation in response to a separate physical activity intervention. These results highlight neural processes associated with successful self-affirmation, and further suggest that key pathways may be amplified in conjunction with prospection."*[12]

❖ Understand: These effects that affirmations have on your mind may be a reason why the Prophet of Allah ﷺ said, *"Speak what is good and acquire gains, or refrain from speaking evil and be safe."*[13]

---

[12] Self-affirmation activates brain systems associated with self-related processing and reward and is reinforced by future orientation

[13] Musnad al-Shihab al-Quda'i 666

Dua

Finally, we have dua, the act of supplicating to Allah. A tool that can bring about profound transformation and fix the scattered pieces of your life. When engaging in dua, you must do so with sincerity, humility, and a deep trust in Allah's Wisdom and Mercy. Rasulullah ﷺ said, *"Nothing is more honorable to Allah Almighty than supplication."*[14]

Then on the flip side, if you feel like you don't need Allah, it's crucial that you take a step back and realize that Allah is in control of every issue. The fact that you think you're independent of Allah in even the smallest of matters is a sign of ignorance and pride. Understand that Allah wants you to turn to Him in times of both difficulty and ease. Rasulullah ﷺ, *"Indeed, he who does not ask Allah, He gets angry with him."*[15] In another narration, he ﷺ said, *"Whoever never asks from Allah, He will be*

---

[14] Sunan al-Tirmidhi 3370
[15] Jami` at-Tirmidhi 3373 - Book 48, Hadith 4

angry with him."[16] So pay heed and trust that Allah will answer your dua, for it is a power unlike any other.

Now before you skip the rest of this section, understand that there is a science to dua as well, but first, understanding how to make dua and learning its spirituality is a must.

The basic dua is organized in the following steps:
1. Raise your hands to Allah, or place your head down in sajdah
2. Praise Allah (SubhanAllah, Alhamdulillah, AllahuAkbar, etc)
3. Send Salawat upon the Prophet ﷺ
4. Seek forgiveness from Allah for both major and minor sins
5. Ask Allah for your needs (Meat of the Dua)

---

[16] Sunan al-Tirmidhi 3373

6. Seek forgiveness from Allah for both major and minor sins
7. Send Salawat upon the Prophet ﷺ
8. Praise Allah (SubhanAllah, Alhamdulillah, AllahuAkbar, etc)
9. End with saying, *Ameen.*

❖ Understand: Dua is a form of worship, because when you make dua, you are reminding yourself that Allah is your Lord and He is your only Aid. You essentially confess to Him that without Him, you have nothing. And that besides Him, you have no one to turn to for your affairs. Rasulullah ﷺ said, *"The supplication (dua) is the essence of worship."*[17] And just like your spirituality, the more you enjoin in good, forbid evil, and seek forgiveness from Allah, the more impactful your dua can become.

---

[17] Jami at-Tirmidhi 3371 - Book 48, Hadith 2

Now bear in mind that the concept of dua is a unique one. While supplication may seem like a spiritual theme that lies beyond comprehension, it's essential to realize that contemporary research on spirituality has begun to shed light on dua as well.

Research Behind Dua:

Manifestation. Whether you think it's a fool's errand or a law that runs the universe, it's crucial you understand that the 'law of manifestation' is based on your brain, your thoughts, and your emotions linking to 'spiritual energy'. At least that's what they say nowadays. Therefore, with our limited technology, it is challenging to uncover concrete evidence for this law, but that doesn't mean there isn't any.

This law essentially states that the more you want something, the more you think about it, and the more you imagine that you already have it, the more likely it is for you to attract it. Some even refer to this 'law of manifestation' as the 'law of attraction'. Many claim that for this law of attraction to work, you must believe it to be true for you to attract the thing you desire most. They claim that the harder you believe, the more likely it is to happen.

However, researchers still need more clarity around this growing idea. They say that you must believe in something to be true in order for it to actually come true.[18] However, what does Islam say about this? More specifically, how does Islam connect this idea of manifestation to dua?

The Prophet ﷺ taught us that when we genuinely believe Allah can unlock a path for us, Allah is far more likely to do it, than if we doubt Him. He ﷺ said that Allah said, *"I am just as My slave thinks I am, (i.e. I am able to do for him what he thinks I can do for him) and I am with him if He remembers Me. If he remembers Me in himself, I too, remember him in Myself; and if he remembers*

---

[18] Understanding The Law of Attraction

Me in a group of people, I remember him in a group that is better than they; and if he comes one span nearer to Me, I go one cubit nearer to him; and if he comes one cubit nearer to Me, I go a distance of two outstretched arms nearer to him; and if he comes to Me walking, I go to him running."[19]

This hadith of Rasulullah ﷺ clearly indicates that the more faith you have in Allah, the more likely it is for you to invoke His blessings and His help. The only caveat is that you must genuinely believe that He is able to unlock your locked doors! And unlike how contemporary researchers vaguely say, *'Believe in something hard enough, and it'll come true,'* the Prophet ﷺ outlined exactly and specifically how to invoke the Help of Allah, by teaching us the concept of dua. Believe that Allah will answer your dua, and InSha'Allah He will, one way or the other.

---

[19] Sahih al-Bukhari 7405 - Book 97, Hadith 34

The Mind: Secrecy

It's natural for you to desire to share your ideas, goals, and achievements with people. Because doing so can create a false sensation of 'feeling good' by receiving praise. However, it's crucial to maintain secrecy and modesty when it comes to Allah's blessings upon you, especially regarding goals you are actively working towards. The less people know, the less they can use against you.

Now you may be thinking, *'Well, I can probably share my ideas with those close to me. They're not going to do anything bad.'* That's where you're wrong. Looking around you, you'll sometimes find that even those closest to you are not always looking out for your best interests. They may secretly envy your success and eagerly await your downfall. It's unfortunate, yet true, that negativity and jealousy exist, especially when Allah blesses you more than them. However, many don't realize it, but jealousy is an emotion that will not only harm the person feeling it, but may also hurt the person it's directed at.

Yes, if someone is jealous of you, that jealousy can affect you. According to Rasulullah ﷺ, jealousy can manifest as the evil eye, known as nazr.

The rest of this chapter will cover the life-threatening effects of nazr, but before we move on, understand that our Rasool ﷺ gave a very simple, yet crucial piece of advice to avoid these issues altogether. He ﷺ said, *"Whoever is silent, he is saved."*[20]

Destruction Through Jealousy

Nazr, also known as the evil eye, is an infection. As a baseline explanation, nazr is created when people are jealous of you or the blessings that Allah bestows you with. For instance, people may be jealous of your clear skin. Someone's nazr on you

---

[20] Jami at-Tirmidhi 2501 - Book 37, Hadith 87

can cause acne and breakouts. People may envy
that new car you just bought. Someone's nazr on
your car can cause an accident, destroying it.
People may even envy your health, potentially
causing your death. The Prophet ﷺ said, *"A great
many from my nation who die, after the judgment,
decree, and providence of Allah, die by the evil
eye."[21]*

In another hadith, Rasulullah ﷺ further
emphasized the devastating impact of the evil eye,
saying that if anything possessed the capability to
influence Allah's decree, it would be nazr. He ﷺ
said, *"The evil eye is real. If anything could precede
the divine decree, it would be preceded by the evil
eye. When you are asked to perform a ritual bath,
then do so."[22]*

---

[21] Musnad Abi Dawud al-Tayalisi 1868
[22] Sahih Muslim 2188

❖ Note: There are ways to protect both yourself from nazr, and others from your nazr. But first, you need to understand that jealousy is a common occurrence in humans. But being good is a choice — wishing the best for others is a choice. So, in order to protect others from your nazr, seek blessings for them. Rasulullah ﷺ said, *"If one of you sees something with his brother that he admires, let him pray for blessing (barakah) for him."*[23]

As to how you should seek blessings for another person, Ibn al-Qayyim says, *"If the one who is looking fears that he could cause harm by his evil eye to the object that he is looking at, then he may ward off its evil by saying "Allahumma barik 'alayhi (O Allah, bless it for him)."*[24]

Then, to protect or cure yourself from the evil eye, Rasulullah ﷺ highlighted certain chapters and verses

---

[23] Imam Ahmad in al-Musnad (25/355)
[24] Zad al-Ma'ad, 4/156

48

from the Quran to recite. This is called *Ruqyah*. Aisha رضي الله عنها said, *"The Messenger of Allah (peace and blessings of Allah be upon him) commanded me, or he commanded (the people) to use ruqyah to deal with the evil eye."*[25] And in another hadith narrated by Aisha رضي الله عنها, the Prophet ﷺ said, *"The man who cast the evil eye would be commanded to do wudoo, and then the man who was affected would wash himself with (the water)."*[26]

Destruction Through The Mind

Now, nazr is in relation to jealousy. But what about the self-destructive consequences that follow when you go about revealing your intentions, goals, and plans to others? How could that impact your productivity? To understand this, you must first learn

---

[25] al-Bukhari, al-Tibb, 5297
[26] Abu Dawood, al-Tibb, 3382. Al-Albani said, in Sahih Sunan Abi Dawud, its isnad is sahih. No. 3282

what dopamine is, and how it relates to revealing your intentions.

Dopamine is essentially the reward chemical in the brain. Numerous cognitive, memory, motivational, and pleasure-related processes depend on dopamine. Since dopamine is a neurotransmitter, it significantly influences feelings of pleasure and reward in response to gratifying events, essentially supporting the brain's pleasure and reward systems. For example, eating exquisite cuisine, participating in enjoyable activities, or hitting the gym, all release dopamine in your body.

This is where both positive and negative habits are formed, such as working out, training, studying, etc. Or on the flip side, the cheap, negative habits, including smoking, drugs, alcohol consumption, etc., can form as well. When you train your body to release dopamine after the positives, you'll watch yourself become more productive in numerous aspects of your life. Because you are essentially training your mind to release dopamine only after you've accomplished difficult tasks. It will become a habit.

On the flip side, when you train your brain to release hits of dopamine after scrolling on social media, consuming intoxicants, or any of the other cheap negatives, you'll find yourself experiencing brain fog, lack of productivity, and overall lack of ambition. Because now, you've trained your brain to reward you without you having to do much.

❖ Note: As mentioned, setting and working towards long-term goals that require dedicated effort can trigger a surge of positive energy in the form of dopamine.

According to Nick Wolny, "*dopamine not only spikes when we set a goal for ourselves but also when we're close to achieving that goal. The bigger the reward, the more powerful the spike. This is probably*

why we're able to power through in a race or a project
once we see light at the end of the tunnel."[27]

However, these bursts of dopamine can very well be replicated by means that will lead to self-destruction apart from the common cheap bursts of dopamine. One of these ways is by blabbering on about your ideas and goals to people before they become a reality.

Based on numerous studies, when you receive admiration and compliments from others before achieving your goals, your brain releases a similar burst of dopamine compared to that you'd receive after completing your tasks. Thus, making you significantly less likely to actually complete your work. In other words, blabbering on about your plans can destroy you.

---

[27] Nick Wolny: Why you love setting goals more than pursuing them, according to science

According to Marwa Azab, PhD, *"The more others admire our goals, the more dopamine rush we get, and the less likely we are to execute the future necessary actions to implement them. Therefore we deplete our 'feel good' gas, keeping us from reaching our final destination: our goal. Furthermore, publicizing our intention to succeed gives us a 'premature sense of completeness'. It signals the brain to move on. If the brain believes that you have reached your goal, it might inhibit the specific brain circuits related to further pursuing this goal."*[28]

Marwa says, *"The more others admire our goals, the more dopamine rush we get."*[29] This is similar to what Rasulullah ﷺ said about over-complimenting people. He ﷺ taught us, that if we genuinely care for someone, we must not over-

[28] Marwa Azab PhD: Why Sharing Your Goals Makes Them Less Achievable
[29] Marwa Azab PhD: Why Sharing Your Goals Makes Them Less Achievable

praise them. Or else we risk ruining their lives. Abu Musa Al-Ashari said, *"The Prophet ﷺ heard someone praising another and exaggerating in his praise. The Prophet ﷺ said, 'You have ruined or cut the man's back (by praising him so much).'"*[30]

---

[30] Sahih al-Bukhari 2663 - Book 52, Hadith 27

Laws of Societal Respect

In a man's quest to establish an honorable and prophetic presence within society, he may often find that building such a reputation requires consistency over the course of months, if not years. But what must he be consistent with? Does he simply just need to offer goodness and positivity to others all the time? The answer is yes, but also no.

Although embodying characteristics such as honesty, truthfulness, kindness, gentleness, mercy, and love, are fundamental aspects of masculinity, you cannot be naive. Understand that although Rasulullah ﷺ was sent as a mercy to mankind, he ﷺ was also a husband, a father, and a leader. He was the founder of the first Islamic state, and overall, he ﷺ was a man. And as a man, our Prophet ﷺ had to maintain respect and honor — societal benefits that a weak and naive man simply cannot attract!

In his masculinity ﷺ, we find the embodiment of two fundamental values a man should embody: respect and influence. Although, in order to attract such values, you must first master the various arts that come into play. For instance, when someone seeks your help, how do you respond? Or when you're walking down the street, how should you carry yourself? And what about your appearance? To what extent should you focus on your physical beauty?

To answer such questions, reflecting upon the life of our Rasool ﷺ is a must. Because both before and after assuming the mantle of prophethood at the age of 40, he ﷺ was always known for his purity. There is no record of him ﷺ ever resorting to unethical actions that would stain a man's image. Even those who encountered him ﷺ without prior knowledge of his exalted status ﷺ, like the Bedouin woman he ﷺ met during the Hijrah, would be moved by his self-respect and dignity.

When the Prophet ﷺ was traveling from Mecca to Medina, he ﷺ and his companions ﷺ took shelter at a camp in an area known as Qudaid. There, they met a bedouin woman who didn't know who he ﷺ was at the time, and yet she described him ﷺ as such: *"I saw a man of visible radiance and purity, beautiful appearance, bright-faced, with neither protruding ribs nor a small head, handsome and fair. His eyes were deep black and large, and his eyelashes were lush. His voice was mellow and soft. The whiteness of his eyes was bright and his pupils were very black. His eyebrows were beautifully arched and connected.*

His neck was long, his beard densely full. When he was silent, he appeared dignified. When he spoke, he was eminent and crowned with magnificence. His speech was sweet, his words precise, neither too little nor too much. Like a string of pearls flowing down gradually.[31]

❖ Understand: This woman, Umm Ma'Bad, had just met the Prophet ﷺ for the first time, not even knowing who he ﷺ was. Yet, she described him ﷺ in such a dignified manner.

Fortunately for us, when we study the life of our Prophet ﷺ, we learn that the very principles found in his manhood ﷺ, are common themes of respect in the modern world. We are able to understand and visualize his teachings ﷺ through examples he ﷺ set for us. And so, as a man, you must quickly understand that to acquire a character like our Rasool ﷺ, you need to learn to speak as he ﷺ spoke, walk as he ﷺ walked, eat as he ﷺ ate, and so forth.

---

[31] Ar-Raheeq Al-Makhtum The Sealed Nectar, P.572 - Zadul-Ma'ad 2/45

Now, in society, there are a plethora of laws out there that you must adhere to in order to attain and, more importantly, maintain respect. So, to provide you with the essentials, this chapter, *Laws of Societal Respect*, will uncover the ten fundamental, yet essential prophetic laws of respect that, if you adhere to them, you will find an almost immediate, positive change in both yourself, and in how others treat you.

Forgiveness

A powerful man is one who is dominating, unforgiving, and feared; at least, that's what the Pagans at the time of Rasulullah ﷺ argued. So when Islam came, contradicting their views and equalizing all mankind, this fear of equality with the 'lower class,' along with men having to show humility, struck the Pagans deeply. Although, indulged in their arrogance, they failed to realize the magnitude of harm their actions were causing to both themselves and society as a whole.

That is why it is crucial to understand that animosity, hatred, and anger, are all aspects that discreetly pierce and rupture the spirit. They disturb one's mental peace and harden the heart. Many argue that holding on to resentment is almost like sipping poison while wishing death upon the other person. Instead, forgive and move on. Because as Al-San'ani said, *"Grudges are malice, enmity, and hatred. Indeed, they are among the great sins, so let them fall away from your hearts and purify your hearts from them."[32]*

❖ Understand: Yes, purifying your heart from malice is a significant practice in Islam. However, the benefits don't just end at achieving self-peace. Rather, when you learn to forgive and look past, your haters might

---

[32] al-Tanwir Sharh al-Jami al-Saghir 5/38

eventually begin melting for you as well. You may find yourself closer to your former enemies than your friends one day.

Ibn Abbas رضي الله عنه said, "*Allah has commanded patience at a time of anger, and forbearance and forgiveness at a time of being wronged. If they do so, Allah will protect them from Satan and subdue their enemies such that they become like dear friends.*"[33]

And, if that isn't incentive enough, then you should fear *not* forgiving others. Yes, *fear* holding grudges in your heart. Because the Prophet ﷺ made it very clear that Allah loves those who forgive one another, while He dislikes those who don't. Consequently, by holding grudges, you risk repelling the Forgiveness of Allah from yourself. Rasulullah ﷺ said, "*The gates of Paradise are opened on Monday and Thursday. Allah forgives every servant who does not associate anything with Him, except a man with enmity between himself and his*

---

[33] Tafsir al-Tabari 41:34

brother. It will be said: 'Delay these two until they reconcile, delay these two until they reconcile, delay these two until they reconcile.'"[34]

As a man, it's still crucial for you to avoid naivety, learn from your mistakes, and distance yourself from those who genuinely intend to harm you. Now if you're thinking to yourself, *'How can I forgive people who have hurt me so many times? Won't they keep wronging me if I keep forgiving them?'* The answer is no. Because forgiving them does not necessarily entail forgetting the past. According to Everett Worthington, PhD, *"One common but mistaken belief is that forgiveness means letting the person who hurt you off the hook. Yet forgiveness is not the same as justice, nor does it require reconciliation..."[35]* Rather, forgiving just means releasing that capsulized anger from within your

---

[34] Sahih Muslim 2565
[35] Kirsten Weir: Forgiveness can improve mental and physical health

heart in hopes that Allah will forgive you. Because Allah says in the Quran:

وَإِن تَعْفُوا وَتَصْفَحُوا وَتَغْفِرُوا فَإِنَّ اللَّهَ غَفُورٌ رَّحِيمٌ ﴿١٤﴾

... And if you forgive and overlook and pardon, then Allah is Most-Forgiving, Very-Merciful.
(Quran 64:14)

However, this matter of forgiving, yet distancing, slightly changes when it comes to your blood relatives. Yes, it's well known that sometimes more harm can come to you from your own family than from others. However, as a follower of Rasulullah ﷺ, look past, and try your best to keep your kin together. Put in the effort, and watch as Allah's blessings shower upon you. Because Rasulullah ﷺ said, *"Anyone who wants to have his provision expanded and his term of life prolonged should maintain ties of kinship."*[36] Of course, don't beg on

---

[36] Al-Adab Al-Mufrad 56 - Book 2, Hadith 10

your knees to keep your family together, losing respect and dignity, but also don't give up as quickly as you would with others.

The Man of Paradise

On one occasion, the Prophet ﷺ was engaged with a few of the sahaba in the masjid when a man was about to enter. In praise of that man, the Prophet ﷺ said, *"A man will now enter who is from the people of Paradise."*

The man walked in a second time, and then a third time, each time the Prophet ﷺ praising him. Now the sahaba who would eagerly strive for the best in both worlds just had to know what made this man so special. Why did the Messenger of Allah ﷺ speak so highly of him? To uncover this mystery, Abdullah ibn Amr ibn al-As رضي الله عنه took action to find out.

Abdullah رضي الله عنه went to this man and told him that he quarreled with his father and needed a place to stay for a few nights. During this time, it was common for people to stay at each other's homes, so the man allowed Abdullah ibn Amr رضي الله عنه to spend a few nights with him.

Abdullah رضي الله عنه noticed that the man didn't perform many extra deeds out of the ordinary. For example, he wasn't always fasting or praying excessively apart from his fard salats, sunnah/nafil, etc. So after three days of living with him, still baffled about what made him so beloved in the Eyes of Allah, Abdullah ibn Amr said to the man, *"O servant of Allah, I have not quarreled with my father nor have I cut relations with him. I heard the Messenger of Allah say three times that a man from the people of Paradise was coming to us, and then you came. So I thought I should stay with you and see what you are doing that I should follow, but I did not see you do anything special. What is the reason that the Messenger of Allah spoke highly of you?"*

The man replied, saying that whatever good he does, is whatever Abdullah had seen. He said, *"It is as you have seen."* Accepting this, as Abdullah ibn Amr رضي الله عنه was about to leave, the man stopped him and said, *"It is as you have seen, except that I do not find fraud in my soul towards the Muslims, and I do not envy anyone because of the good that Allah has given them."[37]*

In another narration of this story, when Abdullah ibn Amr رضي الله عنه asked the man what made him so unique, he replied, *"Every night, before I go to sleep, I forgive whoever has wronged me. I remove any bad feelings towards anyone from my heart."[38]*

❖ Understand: For the Prophet ﷺ to speak about someone in such high regard is considered an honor every Muslim can only dream of. Although, the man who Rasulullah ﷺ spoke about didn't really engage in excessive worship more than the average Muslim

---

[37] Musnad Aḥmad 12286
[38] Kitab al-Zuhd by Ibn al-Mubarak, Number 694

would — he didn't necessarily keep nafil fasts more than the sahaba would, nor would he devote excess time to nafil prayers according to this hadith.

But that one consistent act of forgiveness, that one daily act of spiritual cleansing, allowed him to acquire one of life's greatest honors and rewards — confirmation of paradise from the Prophet ﷺ himself. Ayyub al-Sakhtiyani said, "*A man will not hit the mark, nor fulfill his manhood, until he has two characteristics: Forgiving people and overlooking their faults.*"[39]

So men! Forgive, look past, and move on with your life. Refrain from pettiness that will ruin your manhood, for you truly begin to embody prophetic masculinity only when you relieve your heart from vengeance.

---

[39] al-Muru'ah 106

Science Behind Forgiveness:

When you consider forgiving others, you're most likely thinking of moving on. Your intentions may either be to fix your relationship with the person you're forgiving, or you may be doing it solely to please Allah. But very few times do people think about the sciences behind dropping grudges. You may not realize it, but when you forgive those who wrong you, your body and mind will undergo profound transformations that will lead to a plethora of health-related benefits.

Charlotte Witvliet, a psychologist at Hope College, conducted a study on the correlation between physical health and forgiveness. She asked a group of volunteers to recall times when they were abused, hurt, or mistreated by someone while she monitored various body functions. According to Everett Worthington Jr., PhD, *"...she monitored their blood pressure, heart rate, facial muscle tension, and sweat gland activity."[40]*

Expectedly enough, throughout the experiment, Witvliet found that while the volunteers recalled difficult events, their heart rate sped up, their blood pressure rose, and they began sweating more. Their overall physical arousal rose significantly. Then on the flip side, after Witvliet had instructed them to practice forgiveness, the volunteers experienced yet another significant change — this time, a decrease in their physical arousal. According to Worthington, *"Witvliet also asked her subjects to try to empathize with their offenders or imagine forgiving them. When they practiced forgiveness, their physical arousal coasted downward. They showed no more of a stress reaction than normal wakefulness produces."[41]*

---

[40] Everett Worthington Jr. PhD: The New Science of Forgiveness
[41] Everett Worthington Jr. PhD: The New Science of Forgiveness

Smile

A genuine, widespread smile: the look of beauty and a sign of confidence that alters you internally, while melting those around you psychologically. Not only would our Prophet ﷺ project this beam of beauty from his face ﷺ, but he ﷺ also recommended us to do the same. According to authentic sources, both from Muslims and non-Muslims of the time, the Prophet ﷺ smiled so consistently and genuinely that it was almost impossible to find him ﷺ without it. Abdullah ibn Al-Harith ibn Hazm رضي الله عنه said, *"I have never seen anyone who smiles more than the Prophet does."*[42] And Jarir ibn Abdullah رضي الله عنه said, *"Allah's Messenger (peace and blessings be upon him) never refused me permission to see him*

---

[42] Dr. Ali al-Halawani, Jami at-Tirmidhi 3641 - Book 49, Hadith 37

since I embraced Islam and never looked at me but with a smile.[43]

But why? What's so special about smiling, especially if you're smiling at people you don't even know? Won't it make you look 'weak' or 'awkward'? Well, it could make you appear weak if your smile isn't sincere. However, the prophetic, radiant smile that was wide and genuine, was a form of true masculinity. There was no weakness projected by it, but rather love and mercy. Muhammad ibn al-Nadr said, *"The first part of manhood is a cheerful face. The second part is loving kindness to people."*[44]

Now, it's crucial to recognize that we are not living in the same era as our Prophet ﷺ. Yes, the smile is important, but the Prophet ﷺ was a leader for humanity. His smile ﷺ portrayed itself as a sign of compassion, humility, optimism, gratitude, and love.

---

[43] Dr. Ali al-Halawani, Sahih Muslim 2475b - Book 44, Hadith 194

[44] al-Mujalasah wa Jawahir al-'Ilm 828

It made him ﷺ appear approachable and open to conversation, which was crucial for a man, a Messenger like him ﷺ.

❖ Note: In this sea of people, you must be wary of mistakenly displaying quick, unprophetic smiles that may portray themselves as fake. While the prophetic, widespread smile that induces every muscle in the face is used to attract those around you, a weak, quick, and fake smile will portray insecurity. Thus, savor your smile if you wish to influence others to favor your presence.

Art of Smiling:

Leil Lowndes mentions the story of a girl who inherited her father's business in her book, *How To Talk To Anyone: 92 Little Tricks for Big Success in Relationships*. Lowndes describes the girl as charming, yet only to a certain extent. She was the type of person who would constantly give people quick, not-so-real smiles, which didn't represent much apart from the fact that she was a nice person.

However, after her father passed away and she inherited his business, she learned a different, more effective technique of smiling that helped her land tons of prosperous clients. She learned that when you wait for a second upon meeting someone, and then envelop them with a slow, warm, flooding smile, you create a sense of personalization in that smile, showing your clients that your smile was meant only for them. That split-second delay will then almost immediately win their hearts over.

Lowndes says, *"Don't flash an immediate smile when you greet someone, as though anyone who walked into your line of sight would be the beneficiary. Instead, look at the other person's face for a second. Pause. Soak in their persona. Then let a big, warm, responsive smile flood over your face and overflow into your eyes. It will engulf the recipient like a warm wave. The split-second delay convinces people your flooding smile is genuine and only for them."*[45]

William Shakespeare said, *"It's easier to get what you want with a smile than with the tip of the sword."* I.e., the charm a smile displays will outweigh the fear of a sword, relating to Voltaire's saying: *"Smile melts ice, installs confidence and heals wounds; it's the key of sincere human relations."*[46]

❖ Note: It's crucial to understand that while Lowndes, Shakespeare, and Voltaire may be promoting the idea of smiling as slightly manipulative, studying the appearance of our Prophet ﷺ, we see that with him ﷺ, that wasn't the case. He ﷺ was a man, who, by Allah's will, was able to accumulate thousands of adherents

---

[45] Leil Lowndes: How To Talk To Anyone: 92 Little Tricks for Big Success in Relationships Pg. 8
[46] Dr. Ali Al-Halawani: 5 Prophet's Hadiths About Smiling

during his lifetime, and billions more after his passing ﷺ.

If he ﷺ didn't radiate genuine positivity wherever he ﷺ went, his success would've only lasted him ﷺ so long. Eventually, seduction and manipulation wear off, only leaving behind the true colors of the man playing it. In terms of a smile, you wear it to project a positive outlook that will cause those around you to feel good. I.e., you smile more for them, than for yourself.

Rasulullah ﷺ said, "*Your smiling in the face of your brother is charity...*"[47] Smiling is such an act that it causes both the giver and the receiver to feel uplifted and appreciated. Then, that deed is met with the same reward as charity in the Sight of Allah. So how can we relate this to science?

---

[47] Jami` at-Tirmidhi 1956 - Book 27, Hadith 62

Science Behind Smiling:

You've read the external benefits of smiling, that it impacts those around you, yet there is one more that has to do with your appearance. However, before you read how smiling can impact your appearance, you'll find that adopting a sunny facial look is bound to improve your health as well.

According to Mark Stibich, PhD, smiling can impact a plethora of stress-related issues in your body. Some of these issues that smiling can fix are a lousy mood, high blood pressure, and physical pain. Then, smiling can also help you live longer — yes, smiling may extend your lifespan.

Mark says, *"Happy people seem to enjoy better health and longevity, but more research is needed to understand why. Research indicates that happiness could increase lifespan by years—*

suggesting maintaining a happy, positive mood may be an important part of a healthy lifestyle."[48]

So now that you've learned of all the internal benefits of smiling, here is the last key benefit of smiling that will surely catch your attention: Smiling makes you more attractive. According to a study by Anthony C. Little and his team from the University of Stirling, smiling directly correlates to facial attractiveness when rated by others. They say, *"Expression certainly has large effects, with, for example, faces shown with smiles rated as more attractive and as having more positive personality traits than neutral faces..."[49]*

❖ Note: When you only mask a neutral, bland face, people can perceive you as dull, unapproachable,

---

[48] Mark Stibich, PhD: 10 Big Benefits of Smiling: Choose to smile every day to boost mood and health
[49] Anthony C. Little: Facial attractiveness: evolutionary based research

boring, etc. And vice-versa! Yet, if you are still unsure whether you should carry a smile or not, just remember that, if nothing else, smiling will at least portray you as someone approachable and open to conversation — so long as your smile is genuine and legit.

Mentorship

To mentor well, you must first see the struggles of the one who seeks to be. Offer guidance with a heart of love, and let compassion guide your glove. Teach with patience and empathy, and inspire with gentle honesty. Remember, the path to success is paved with hard work and finesse. Encourage growth, embrace the change, and celebrate the progress made. So lead with kindness, mercy, and care, and see the beauty that will appear. In the journey of mentorship lies the power to transform and uplift.

As a man, there are a plethora of masculine aspects that you must uphold. And perhaps mentorship is one of the most crucial ones. For it is through mentorship that you can truly make a difference in the lives of those around you. But make no mistake; mentorship is not an easy task. It is a fragile endeavor that requires selflessness, openness, and a willingness to help those surrounding you without expecting anything in return.

Be the mentor, the friend who will inspire them of Islam. Be the man who will inspire others to follow the teachings of your Prophet ﷺ.

And in order to uplift those around you, work to befriend those who have no friends, sacrifice your time for those who need it more than you, and believe that through your selfless actions, Allah will be the One to help you in your times of need. Because when you help others at their low, Allah will help you, regardless of your needs, InSha'Allah. Rasulullah ﷺ said, *"Allah continues to fulfill the needs of the servant as long as he fulfills the needs of his brother."[50]*

❖ Note: Before we move on with the rest of this chapter, exploring the effects your social circle can have on you is crucial. As Rasulullah ﷺ said, your religion and your identity will be based on your friends. He ﷺ said, *"A man follows the religion of his friend; so each one should consider whom he makes his friend."[51]* They influence you, and you influence them. Therefore, as an ambitious man chasing success, it is crucial for you to identify what sort of people you want to influence you. This is something you'll need to sit back and contemplate.

Although, as a general rule of thumb, you will want friends who are focused on different aspects of life

---

[50] al-Mu'jam al-Kabir 4664
[51] Sunan Abi Dawud 4833 - Book 43, Hadith 61

that fall under your ambitions. I personally maintain five types of friends in my inner circle.[52]

1. A friend who will inspire me to follow the Commands of Allah and the teachings of Rasulullah ﷺ. As humans, we will naturally fall into sin and slip off our deen. Having a friend or two who can correct your sins and help bring you back on track is always crucial. Rasulullah ﷺ said, *"A man follows the religion of his friend; so each one should consider whom he makes his friend."*[53]

2. A friend involved in business. Having a friend who's always talking about business in your inner circle will give you someone to bounce ideas off when it comes to wealth. If he is ambitious and constantly discussing new ways

---

[52] The following list was created by this book's co-author Azhaan Mohammed
[53] Sunan Abi Dawud 4833 - Book 43, Hadith 61

to make money, you'll eventually catch on and begin working towards financial freedom as well. Allah says in the Quran:

فَإِذَا قُضِيَتِ الصَّلَاةُ فَانتَشِرُوا فِي الْأَرْضِ وَابْتَغُوا مِن فَضْلِ اللَّه

Once the prayer is over, disperse throughout the land and seek the bounty of Allah.

(Quran 62:10)

3. A friend involved in deen work. Now this is different from a friend who is just religious. This friend uses the teachings of Islam to impact and influence lives. He will be putting himself out there by working to better the lives of others. Perhaps he will be on the streets helping the homeless, or constantly looking for philanthropic projects to take on. Regardless, having a friend like him will present you with opportunities to get involved in your community

as well. Rasulullah ﷺ said, *"The best of people are those who are most beneficial to people."*[54]

4. A friend who will push you to take care of your body. This is mainly in terms of fitness. He should be someone who will guide your progress in the gym, push you when you're slacking off, and overall inspire you to become the best version of yourself physically. Rasulullah ﷺ said, *"The strong believer is more beloved to Allah than the weak believer, but there is goodness in both of them."*[55]

5. A friend focused on school. This friend should be more dedicated than you when it comes to studies. He will inspire you to stay on track in terms of your academics, regardless of what field you're studying. Because, as a Muslim,

---

[54] al-Mu'jam al-Awsat 5937
[55] Sahih Muslim 2664 - Introduction, Hadith 224

seeking knowledge is mandatory upon you. Rasulullah ﷺ said, *"Seeking knowledge is an obligation upon every Muslim."[56]*

Going back to mentorship, you must understand that, as with any work devoted toward the greater good, there are crucial pitfalls to avoid. When it comes to mentorship, you must learn to assess both the situation and the person before offering your help. Even with the best intentions, your approach to someone's situation can either foster a bond of trust, or simply cause that person to draw away from you.

And when you do decide to offer guidance, remember to keep your advice sincere, especially when they seek your help first. If you become too used to sugarcoating your advice, not only will you not be of much benefit to the people, but you may also fall into the sin of lying — essentially destroying

---

[56] Sunan Ibn Majah 224

your manhood. Ahnaf ibn Qais رضي الله عنه said, *"There is no manhood for the liar."*[57]

❖ Understand: People can sense when someone is being insincere or disingenuous. So as a man of respect, be honest, direct, and true to the person you are mentoring. Al-Qashani said, *"Sincere advice is the desire for good for people, making clear for them the path of righteousness and piety, aspiring to benefit them, and not desiring harm for them."*[58] Imam Ali ibn Abi Talib رضي الله عنه also said, *"Sincere advice is from the noble traits of character."*[59]

Now, what about the different forms of giving advice? And how can you start advising people without worrying about how they'll take it? One

---

[57] Shu'ab al-Iman 6123
[58] Al-Qashani, Abad al-Tariqah wa Asrar al-Haqiqah fi Risa'il al-Sheikh Abd al-Razzaq al-Qashani, p.33, Dawud Walid: Futuwwah
[59] Al-Tamimi, Ghurar al-Hikam wa Durar al-Kalim, p.357, Dawud Walid: Futuwwah

general, yet effective method is to simply break the ice with *'Hey, I noticed you doing such and such. Can I give you some advice?'* More often than not, their answer will be *sure*, and they'll find your advice coming off as sincere.

Now what does it mean to always be sincere, and how can you apply that sincerity to your mentorship? One way is to simply advise people, where you don't actively look towards building a relationship with them. You merely convey your point with sincerity, understanding, and, most importantly, humility. Then you move on.

Although, what if you wish to build new connections, or already have an ongoing relationship with them? What should you do in these cases where you may overthink more in order to avoid hurting the person? To illuminate your questions, the following three stories in this subchapter will explain how the prophet ﷺ advised three different categories of people, in three different scenarios based on their personalities. By studying the following stories, can you get an idea of how the Prophet ﷺ would correct those around him ﷺ.

The Extended Salat

Learning to recognize the different qualities within people before spreading your knowledge is crucial. For instance, advising elders, leaders, or people of knowledge can differ from advising youngsters and peers. We see this when Allah commanded Musa عليه السلام to speak gently when he approached Firaun, who was a prideful and tyrannical leader of the time. Allah said in the Quran:

فَقُولَا لَهُ قَوْلًا لَّيِّنًا لَّعَلَّهُ يَتَذَكَّرُ أَوْ يَخْشَى ﴿٤٤﴾

Speak to him gently, so perhaps he may be mindful [of Me] or fearful [of My] punishment`
(Quran 20:44)

This form of gentle correction will differ, however, when you are approaching people with more knowledge. If the advice you seek to offer them is deen-related, then you may need to act differently depending on the situation and the person. An example we find from the life of Rasulullah ﷺ in regard to correcting someone of knowledge, is found in the story of Mu'adh ibn Jabal رضي الله عنه.

Mu'adh ibn Jabal رضي الله عنه was a great scholar and an Ansar, placing him at a significant standing in the Eyes of Allah. On one occasion, however, Mu'adh was leading the prayers when he began reciting lengthy surahs, potentially causing those praying behind him discomfort for having to stand for so long.

One of the sahaba praying behind him couldn't bear the lengthy salat, so he left his prayer behind Mu'adh, and prayed alone. After the prayer, when Mu'adh ibn Jabal was informed of this man's actions, he said, *"Tomorrow I will mention that to the Messenger of Allah ﷺ."*

The next day, Mu'adh رضي الله عنه went to the Prophet ﷺ and complained of the incident. So the Prophet ﷺ sent for the man who left the prayer and asked him, *"What made you do what you did?"*

He replied to the Prophet ﷺ saying, *"O Messenger of Allah ﷺ, I had been working with my camel to bring water all day, and when I came, the Iqamah for prayer had already been said, so I entered the Masjid and joined him in the prayer, then he recited such and such a Surah and made it lengthy, so I went away and prayed in a corner of the Masjid."* The Prophet ﷺ then turned to Mu'adh رضي الله عنه and, with a strict tone, exclaimed three times:

"Oh Mu'adh are you someone who causes fitnah! Oh Mu'adh are you someone who causes fitnah! Oh Mu'adh are you someone who causes fitnah!"[60]

---

[60] Sunan an-Nasa'i 831 - Book 10, Hadith 55. Note: The word *Fitnah* in this context refers to causing undue hardship, discord, or division between the Muslims.

Our Prophet ﷺ then instructed Mu'adh رضي الله عنه to lead the prayer with short passages and chapters from the Quran when he leads others, while considering the people's circumstances and weaknesses. I.e., do not lengthen the prayers so much that the people dread coming to the masjid or praying in a congregation.

❖ Note: We understand that the Prophet ﷺ was direct and strict here because he ﷺ understood that Mu'adh رضي الله عنه was a knowledgeable scholar of Islam. Being blunt and strict with him would only push him to improve and refine his actions to serve society better and obey Allah.

However, be very careful when applying this method of mentorship, because there is a fine line between nudging people towards greatness and breaking them. Never insult or humiliate those around you, thinking it's for their best, because you will be wrong. Rather, according to Ibn al-Mubarak, your manhood will be corrupted when you belittle those around you. Ibn al-Mubarak said, *"Whoever belittles his brothers will lose his manhood."*[61]

❖ Note: Do not go about being stern like you read in this example of the Prophet ﷺ to people who are older, and especially more knowledgeable than you. If you see a genuine mistake, depending on your relationship with them, consider seeking their advice first. Then, as you listen to them, instead of directly telling them to change their ways, ask them about the situation or issue in more detail. Then, as they explain, consider putting in your own thoughts. This way, they'll catch what you have to say without facing direct opposition. However, this is under the assumption that you carry sufficient knowledge in the field that you are correcting them in.

---

[61] Siyar A'lam al-Nubala' 17/251

The Black Stone

When advising your friends or peers, you understand them. At times you may even be able to predict their next words or actions. Therefore, as their friend, the burden of pushing them towards their full potential by correcting their faults so they may grow, can oftentimes fall on your shoulders. Imam Ali رضي الله عنه said, *"The true friend is he who protects you, advises you regarding your faults, protects you in your absence, and gives to you over himself."*[62]

Usually, when it comes to your friends, depending on the strength of your relationship, there is no need to shy away from being bland with them. You can avoid sugarcoating your advice unless being bland and strict will cause more harm than good to them. The Prophet ﷺ said, *"The believer is a*

---

[62] Al-Tamimi, Ghurar al-Hikam wa Durar al-Kalim, p.175, Dawud Walid: Futuwwah

mirror to his faithful brother. He protects him against loss and defends him behind his back"[63]

On one occasion, our Prophet ﷺ was by the Kaaba, which is always crowded with Muslims praying and circulating it, as this is the House of Allah. So there, he ﷺ saw Umar ibn al-Khattab رضي الله عنه, trying to kiss the Black Stone located on one of the walls of the Kaaba.

As Muslims, we acknowledge that this black stone came down by Allah as a piece of Jannah (paradise) and that by kissing it, Allah will forgive all of our past sins. However, Umar رضي الله عنه was a physically big and strong sahaba. And perhaps he was unintentionally pushing and shoving the people around him in an effort to kiss the Stone. So when Rasulullah ﷺ noticed Umar رضي الله عنه harming those around him, he ﷺ stopped Umar رضي الله عنه and

---

[63] al-Adab al-Mufrad 239

pointed out his flaw. Now the interesting part is, how the Prophet ﷺ did it.

Rasulullah ﷺ said to Umar رضي الله عنه, *"O Umar, you are a strong man. Do not crowd others to touch the Black Stone, lest you harm the weak. If you find a gap, then touch it, otherwise, turn to face it and say La ilaha illallah, and Allahu Akbar."[64]*

❖ Lesson:

1. Rasulullah ﷺ first personalized and acknowledged Umar's name, saying: **"O Umar."**

   As humans, we love the sound of our name. Therefore, mentioning someone's name in your conversation with them, can subconsciously create softness and respect in their mind for you. In turn, they'll be more receptive to your advice. According to Jodi Schulz, acknowledging the other person's name

---

[64] Musnad Ahmad 190 - Book 2, Hadith 107. Note: La ilaha illallah translates to "There is no god but Allah" and Allahu Akbar translates to, "Allah is the greatest."

can create a respectful and comfortable atmosphere. She says, *"Using a person's name in conversation has several benefits. It creates a culture of respect, recognition and consideration for the discussion."*[65]

2. After mentioning Umar's name, he ﷺ acknowledged one of Umar's positive traits, saying: **"You are a strong man."**

    No one likes to hear criticism right off the bat. Instead, even if they're close to you, you want to avoid putting them in a defensive mindset. According to Michael Sorensen, when you validate others before correcting their mistakes, you essentially open their hearts to your words. Thus heavily reducing the chances of your advice being taken the wrong way.

    He says, *"Validation is, in essence, the act of helping someone feel heard and understood. It has the power to calm fears and concerns, add a boost to joy and*

---

[65] Jodi Schulz: Using a person's name in conversation

excitement, avoid or quickly resolve arguments, make people much more open to your advice, and much more. "[66]

3. Then, after easing the situation, the Prophet ﷺ finally corrected Umar's mistake, saying: **"Do not crowd others to touch the Black Stone, lest you harm the weak."**

4. Lastly, after correcting the mistake, Rasulullah ﷺ provided a solution to the issue. He ﷺ said: **"If you find a gap, then touch it, otherwise, turn to face it and say La ilaha illallah, and Allahu Akbar."**

While fulfilling the social needs of your peers is important, it's equally vital to maintain simplicity. Avoiding extremism is a significant aspect of mentorship. As a man, you must give up extremism

---

[66] Michael S. Sorensen: Validation: The Most Powerful Relationship Skill You Were Never Taught

in your faith, work, and especially your dealings with people. Instead, try to understand the burdens and situations of your peers and those around you. Work to access their mind and uncover their truth. Then use that information to improve your mentorship.

If you try building them too quickly and aggressively, you risk them dropping their goals, and falling short of their full potential. They may quickly burn out. And one of the primary faults when being extreme in your mentorship, and consequently in your faith, is that extremism may lead you to correct your brother's mistakes in public out of anger or ego. You will end up humiliating them, not mentoring them. And as a general rule of thumb, even if the mistake you are correcting is public, advise them privately, although the matter has been in public.

Our Prophet ﷺ said, *"Whoever admonishes his brother in private has been sincere to him and*

protected his reputation. Whoever admonishes him
in public has humiliated him and betrayed him."[67]

Now, maintaining privacy augments in weight when
mistakes turn into consistent sins. If your brother
falls into a private sin you discover, you must deal
with them privately. Do not expose their faults. The
feat of publicly correcting someone carries an
element of cruelty, portraying a lack of compassion
and understanding. Conversely, if you were to
disclose another's private transgression to the
public, you risk facing exposure of your sins by Allah
in return.

The Prophet ﷺ said, *"O you who have faith with
their tongues but faith has not entered their hearts!
Do not backbite the Muslims or seek their faults.
Whoever seeks their faults, Allah will seek his faults.*

---

[67] Hilyat al-Awliya 13854

*And if Allah seeks his faults, **He will expose him even in the privacy of his own house.***"[68]

It is worth noting, however, that while advising one another is crucial for an honest society, there were also instances when the Prophet ﷺ chose to withhold his criticism for the betterment of his people ﷺ, as seen during the battle of Uhud.

Uhud

After the Muslims had established Medina as their state, under the leadership of Rasulullah ﷺ, a battle occurred between the Meccans and the Muslims in the year 624 AD, known as the Battle of Badr. In this battle, for every Muslim, there were three Meccans. So it was a definitely a difficult battle for the Muslims, to say the least. Regardless, in the end, victory belonged to the Muslims.

---

[68] Sunan Abi Dawud 4880

However, this wasn't simply a battle between two states, but rather a war between religions. When the Muslims had won, it brought anger and shame to the polytheists of Mecca. They began to fear that their people would begin questioning who God stood with. So to exact revenge and prove to the people otherwise, the Meccans spent a year building their army, gathering weaponry and horses. And by the end of the year, the Meccans stood with an army of three thousand strong, ready to attack, while the Muslims consisted of around seven hundred men ready to defend. It wasn't long until the Prophet ﷺ learned about the incoming threat, to which he ﷺ declared, *"We will meet the approaching enemy at the mountain of Uhud."*

Now Uhud was positioned to the backs of the Muslims. And behind the mountain (the large hill) was a pass. So to avoid the enemy from using that pass and attacking the Muslims from their rear, Rasulullah ﷺ instructed a group of his companions to hold the hill using their bows to ensure that the enemy remained unable to circulate. The Prophet ﷺ also clearly instructed them to remain in their positions whether the Muslims were winning or losing the battle. He ﷺ said to the archers, *"Drive off the horses from us by mean of arrows, lest they should attack us from behind (the rear). Whether we win the battle or lose it, stand steadily in your position and mind that we are not attacked from your side."*[69]

He ﷺ added, *"Defend our backs! If you see us slain, do not come to assist us; and if you see that we have acquired booty, do not share in that with us."*[70]

However, the archers overlooked this advice in the heat of the battle, and just as the Meccans were about to retreat, they rushed ahead into battle, leaving their post. As a result of this mistake, the

---

[69] Ibn Hisham 2/65, 66
[70] Recorded by Ahmed, At-Tabarani, Al-Hakim, Fathul-Bari 7/350

Meccans were then able to encircle the hill of Uhud and reverse the battle at the last minute.

Very soon, in all the chaos of the battle, when it had appeared that the Prophet ﷺ died, the Meccans received their satisfaction and returned, proclaiming their victory. Although the Prophet ﷺ survived, the Muslims faced heavy losses, including the loss of Rasulullah's uncle ﷺ, Hamzah رضي الله عنه, and many others.

Seeing the situation, the archers who abandoned their position at Mount Uhud were prepared for some sort of punishment from the Prophet ﷺ. However, he ﷺ understood there was no need to punish them, considering that they had already understood the cost of their mistake. So with his mercy ﷺ and understanding of the bigger picture, he ﷺ forgave them and moved on, never reminding them of their mistake again. Allah describes the situation in the Quran when He says:

فَبِمَا رَحْمَةٍ مِّنَ اللهِ لِنتَ لَهُمْ وَلَوْ كُنتَ فَظًّا غَلِيظَ الْقَلْبِ لَانفَضُّواْ مِنْ حَوْلِكَ ۖ فَاعْفُ عَنْهُمْ وَاسْتَغْفِرْ لَهُمْ وَشَاوِرْهُمْ فِي الْأَمْرِ ۖ فَإِذَا عَزَمْتَ فَتَوَكَّلْ عَلَى اللهِ ۚ إِنَّ اللهَ يُحِبُّ الْمُتَوَكِّلِينَ ﴿١٥٩﴾

So by mercy from Allah, [O Muhammad], you were lenient with them. And if you had been rude [in speech] and harsh in heart, they would have disbanded from about you. So pardon them and ask forgiveness for them and consult them in the matter. And when you have decided, then rely upon Allah. Indeed, Allah loves those who rely [upon Him].
(Quran 3:159)

❖ Understand: The Muslims were a small group living in the city of Medina. Every man they lost was a heavy loss for the overall religion. And the archers who disobeyed the Prophet ﷺ caused the deaths of so many Muslims, including that of Hamzah رضي الله عنه, the beloved uncle of our Prophet ﷺ. Regardless,

Rasulullah ﷺ still forgave and moved on. And he ﷺ did in the best of ways.

As Allah says in the Quran, not only did he ﷺ forgive them and seek forgiveness on their behalf from Allah, but he ﷺ also ensured to include them in societal matters. Allah commanded him ﷺ to consult with them, as he ﷺ would with others.

And so, knowing that it'd be better to dismiss than to punish or lecture in this situation, he ﷺ used logic and understanding over negative emotions, further improving society as a whole.

Humor

We delve into the topic of joking with reverence and respect. The laws of Islam, as taught by our Prophet ﷺ, guide us in the ways of speech and humor. For in balance and moderation lies wisdom. But let us not forget the weight of words, for they possess the power to both harm and heal. In this subchapter, we will explore the teachings and wisdom, backed by science and psychology, on the etiquette of joking as taught by our Rasool ﷺ.

For a man who is tirelessly working towards the greater good, it becomes vital for him to establish a positive social hierarchy that places him above his adherents. However, such a hierarchy must not be attained through an ugly character of arrogance, or through malice. Instead, a man's presence must be characterized by love and respect, positively influencing those around him.

We find that the Prophet ﷺ naturally attracted power and influence in his life ﷺ through this gentle and nurturing character, which wasn't common in men of his era. His soft character ﷺ complimented his effective communication skills ﷺ, which relied heavily on his ability ﷺ to maintain dignity and respect. And in order to maintain that societal respect, one of the key aspects of demeanor that the Prophet ﷺ paid very close attention to was his humor ﷺ.

Studies confirm that one's sense of humor is a crucial aspect of their character, reflecting who they truly are. Therefore, it is vital to use humor in a positive way, making people feel valued instead of causing them to resent you. To practically apply this in your life, Rasulullah ﷺ established ground rules for playful interactions with others, emphasizing the importance of upholding dignity in all situations. So what are the laws of humor outlined by the prophetic teachings?

- **Do Not Make Fun of Islam:**
  Understand that when you joke about the rules of Islam, you are opening the doors to receive disrespect from others by watering down your religion. And this constitutes a grave error, because Allah says in the Quran:

وَلَئِن سَأَلْتَهُمْ لَيَقُولُنَّ إِنَّمَا كُنَّا نَخُوضُ وَنَلْعَبُ قُلْ أَبِاللهِ وَآيَاتِهِ وَرَسُولِهِ كُنتُمْ

تَسْتَهْزِؤُونَ ﴿٦٥﴾

If you ask them (about this), they declare:
"We were only talking idly and joking." Say:
"Was it at Allah, and His verses and His
Messenger that you were mocking?"
(Quran 9:65)

لاَ تَعْتَذِرُواْ قَدْ كَفَرْتُم بَعْدَ إِيمَانِكُمْ

Make no excuse; you disbelieved after you had
believed.
(Quran 9:66)

- **Do Not Lie Even When Joking:**
Rasulullah ﷺ said, *"Woe to the one who talks*
about something to make the people laugh, in
which he lies. Woe to him! Woe to him!"[71] And the
Prophet ﷺ warned against this form of humor

---

[71] Jami at-Tirmidhi 2315 - Book 36, Hadith 12

which some jokers are accustomed to. He ﷺ said, *"Verily, a man might speak a word to make those around him laugh, yet by it he plunges farther than the star of Pleiades."[72]*

Science Behind Lying:

Deception, no matter how minor, always attracts consequences that will catch up to you sooner or later. Not only will you lose the trust and respect of those around you, but the negative psychological impact of lying can be profound.

Constantly deceiving people can lead to an increased risk of cancer, obesity, anxiety, depression, addiction, gambling, poor work satisfaction, and poor relationships, just to list a few.[73]

And one of the key reasons lying leads to such problems is mainly due to the stress that lying

---

[72] Musnad Ahmad 9220
[73] Chris Iliades, MD: The Truth About Lies

creates in your body. Yes, when you lie, whether you realize it or not, it creates a sense of stress, and if that stress builds up over long periods of time, it could be detrimental to your health. Chris Iliades, MD, states, *"Lying is taxing both physically and emotionally. Because one lie leads to another, you can be forced into a nerve-wracking cycle of lies that becomes harder and harder to keep track of. Long-term exposure to stress can lead to serious health problems and can decrease longevity."*[74]

On the flip side of this negative deceit, by prioritizing integrity in your words and actions, you not only strengthen your relationships with others, but also enhance your own mental and physical well-being. Do not allow deception to weigh you down — embrace honesty as a way of life.

---

[74] Chris Iliades, MD: The Truth About Lies

- **Do Not Frighten Others:**

  Abu Layla رضي الله عنه said, *"The companions of Muhammad ﷺ said that they were traveling with the Prophet ﷺ, and a man among them fell asleep. Some of them got a rope and tied him up, and he got scared.* The Messenger of Allah ﷺ said, *'It is not permissible for a Muslim to frighten another Muslim.'"*[75]

Science Behind Frightening People:

Nobody enjoys being laughed at, especially not after being humiliated by a scare. However, following the trend set by our Prophet ﷺ, frightening people for a laugh may also bring about health problems. These are usually due to what's known as the fight-or-flight response. According to Dr. Michael Castine, a cardiologist at

---

[75] Abd Al-Malik Al-Qaasim: What Are the Conditions of Joking in Islam? Narrated by Abu Dawood

Ochsner Medical Center, *"When you experience fear, your body prepares itself for prompt action by triggering your "fight-or-flight" response. This response begins in a region of your brain called the hypothalamus, which sounds the alarm and triggers increased production of adrenaline in your adrenal glands. That's the rush you feel when scared."*[76]

He says while the overall adrenaline rush your body experiences could be good for you to an extent, if you have pre-existing health problems relating to the heart, the effects of that rush could be fatal.

- **Do Not Mock Others:**
  Avoid hurting people with defaming words, winking behind their backs, or making insulting remarks about them. Allah says in the Quran:

---

[76] Michael Castine, MD: Can Being Scared Be Good for Your Health?

يَا أَيُّهَا الَّذِينَ آمَنُوا لَا يَسْخَرْ قَومٌ مِّن قَوْمٍ عَسَى أَن يَكُونُوا خَيْرًا مِّنْهُمْ وَلَا نِسَاء مِّن نِّسَاء عَسَى أَن يَكُنَّ خَيْرًا مِّنْهُنَّ وَلَا تَلْمِزُوا أَنفُسَكُمْ وَلَا تَنَابَزُوا بِالْأَلْقَابِ

Oh you who believe! Let not a group scoff at another group, it may be that the latter are better than the former. Nor let (some) women scoff at other women, it may be that the latter are better than the former. Nor defame one another, nor insult one another by nicknames.
(Quran 49:11)

Psychology Behind Mocking People:

This is a matter of simply maintaining your respect and dignity. When you mock and humiliate others in public, you may get a couple of laughs or giggles from others. However, doing so consistently and regularly will not only destroy your public respect and image, but may also cause your victim to grow resentment towards you.

- **Limit Your Humor:**
Controlling both your laughter and jokes is a key law of respect taught by both Rasulullah ﷺ and psychology. As humans, you may feel good about speaking excessively, but the person who is being forced to listen to you may find it irritating. Now connect that to humor. Sure, in some instances, if you're genuinely funny, people may enjoy listening to you crack jokes all night. However, is that really something you want?

As both a Muslim and a man, it's crucial for you to maintain balance in your life — even in terms of joking. Don't be that one guy whose sole purpose is to make others laugh by any means. In doing so, you will eventually allow others to walk all over you. They'll begin to view you as someone who is attention-seeking or weak-minded. According to Jared Pistoia, *"Similarly, when using the self-defeating style, others may lose respect for you or have difficulty taking you seriously."*[77]

Here, Pistoia backs Rasulullah's words ﷺ on limited humor. Rasulullah ﷺ said, *"Laugh little. Much laughter kills the heart."*[78] And in another narration, the Prophet ﷺ said, *"And laugh little, for laughing a lot deadens the heart."*[79]

Although, when you're planning on implementing Rasulullah's advice ﷺ on this matter, it'd be good to visualize what his laughter ﷺ would look and sound like.

To give you a description, Abdullah ibn al-Harith رضي الله عنه said that the laughter of Rasulullah ﷺ was inaudible. It was simply just a wider smile than usual. He says, *"The laughter of Allah's Messenger (Allah bless him and give him*

---

[77] Jared C. Pistoia: Humor as a Coping Mechanism
[78] Al-Adab Al-Mufrad 252 - Book 12, Hadith 15
[79] Sunan Ibn Majah 4217 - Book 37, Hadith 118

peace) was nothing but a joyful smile."[80] Then you'll find Ibn Jaz رضي الله عنه saying, *"The laughter of the Messenger of Allah ﷺ was not but smiling."*[81]

- **Do Not Overlap Backbiting With Joking:**
  Understand that backbiting is one of the easiest ways to ruin your reputation in this world, along with attaining horrors in the Hereafter. And one of those horrors was revealed to us by Rasulullah ﷺ after he ﷺ visited the Heavens. Rasulullah ﷺ said, *"During the Mi'raj (the Night of Ascension), I saw a group of people who were scratching their chests and faces with their copper nails. I asked, 'Who are these people, O Jibril?' Jibril replied: 'These are the people who ate flesh of others (by backbiting) and trampled people's honour.'"*[82]

---

[80] Ash-Shama'il Al-Muhammadiyah 227 - Book 34, Hadith 3
[81] Jami at-Tirmidhi 3642 - Book 49, Hadith 38
[82] Riyad as-Salihin 1526 - Book 17, Hadith 16

The prophet ﷺ said, *"He who believes in Allah and the Last Day must either speak good or remain silent."*[83] And to further assert the harsh reality of backbiting, Allah says in the Quran:

يَا أَيُّهَا الَّذِينَ آمَنُوا اجْتَنِبُوا كَثِيرًا مِّنَ الظَّنِّ إِنَّ بَعْضَ الظَّنِّ إِثْمٌ وَلَا تَجَسَّسُوا وَلَا يَغْتَب بَّعْضُكُم بَعْضًا أَيُحِبُّ أَحَدُكُمْ أَن يَأْكُلَ لَحْمَ أَخِيهِ مَيْتًا فَكَرِهْتُمُوهُ

O you who have believed, avoid much [negative] assumption. Indeed, some assumption is sin. And do not spy or backbite each other. Would one of you like to eat the flesh of his brother when dead? You would detest it.
(Quran 49:12)

Science Behind Backbiting:

First off, when you gossip, you reveal a critical flaw within yourself... Or sometimes even multiple

---

[83] Riyad as-Salihin 1511 - Book 17, Hadith 1

flaws. When you talk badly behind someone's back, it's usually because you have nothing better to talk about, or you envy the person you're dishonoring.

In some cases, you could even be backbiting to gain people's attention. Regardless, without realizing it, you are revealing disgusting aspects of your character to the people. According to Sherri Gordon, *"When teens are envious of another person's looks, popularity, or money, they might use gossip and rumors to hurt that person. They also tend to use gossip and rumors to get back at someone who they feel deserves to be hurt. Making up a rumor or spreading gossip sometimes satisfies their need for revenge."*[84]

Gordon also mentions that teens backbite to receive attention or acceptance from a particular group of people. She says, *"...they are the first*

---

[84] Sherri Gordon: Understanding the Impact of Rumors and Gossip

person in the group to hear a rumor, it makes them the center of attention."[85]

And to further go on, tapping into the evils of backbiting doesn't stop exposing your character just yet. It also signifies that if you are so comfortable putting others down in front of your friends, wouldn't you also be capable of putting your friends down in front of others?

Those around you can easily catch on to this when conversing with you. They'll ask themselves, *'Does he really enjoy putting others down for a good laugh? Why is he always so negative?'* It's almost an instant killer for your dignity if you are caught carrying such characteristics. While you may think the people are enjoying your gossip with you, they may actually steer clear of trusting and respecting you.

---

[85] Sherri Gordon: Understanding the Impact of Rumors and Gossip

So to maintain your dignity, refrain from ruining others for the sake of ugly, temporary pleasure.

❖ Understand: Every one of these laws of humor contains wisdom, while some go far as to be backed by science and psychology. While Allah knows best the complete reasoning behind these laws of respect, following them will undoubtedly benefit you. And while rejecting some prophetic laws of humor only brings you dishonor, breaking others, such as backbiting, are counted as major sins to such an extent, that the Prophet ﷺ said, *"The most hateful of you to Allah are those who spread gossip, who cause discord between loved ones and seek misery for the innocent."*[86]

So it's up to you to decide whether to follow the prophetic laws or not. But undoubtedly, choosing to

---

[86] al-Mu'jam al-Awsat 7693

adhere to these laws of joking will lead you to a more honored presence in society.

Generosity

وَأَنفِقُواْ فِي سَبِيلِ اللهِ وَلاَ تُلْقُواْ بِأَيْدِيكُمْ إِلَى التَّهْلُكَةِ وَأَحْسِنُوَاْ إِنَّ اللهَ يُحِبُّ الْمُحْسِنِينَ ﴿١٩٥﴾

Spend in the cause of Allah and do not let your own hands throw you into destruction [by withholding]. And do good, for Allah certainly loves the good-doers.
(Quran 2:195)

We delve into the essence of generosity. The teachings of our Prophet ﷺ that guide us towards the path of selflessness and compassion. For in giving of ourselves, we receive the greatest reward, and in spreading love and kindness, we find true fulfillment. In this subchapter, we will explore the laws and principles of generosity in Islam, from the simple act of smiling at someone to the act of giving away one's wealth to the poor.

A man provides, helps, and serves his community whether they seek his aid or not, similar to a leader who is in service to his people. A true man of authority is not he who terrifies and commands his adherents with brutality. Rather he is one who responds to both the goodness and the evil of society with mercy. Not only will this push his adherents to view him with respectful and trusting eyes, but it may also cause his enemies to overturn their harsh feeling towards him. Imam Ali رضي الله عنه said, *"The kindness of a person and his generosity may make him beloved to his adversaries."*[87]

---

[87] Al-Tamimi, Ghurar al-Hikam wa Durar al-Kalim, p.153, Dawud Walid: Futuwwah

A man must understand that the powerful one isn't demanding, but rather giving. And when you study the life of our Rasool ﷺ, you'll find precisely that. There is hardly a recorded incident when he ﷺ refused aid to anyone seeking it. Jabir ibn Abdullah رضي الله عنه said, *"It never happened that the Messenger of Allah ﷺ was asked for anything and said, 'No.'"*[88]

Adding on this, Al-Hasan ibn 'Ali رضي الله عنه narrated, *"If someone asked him ﷺ for something he needed, he would not send him away without what he had requested, or at least some comforting words. His munificence and his good nature encompassed people such that he became a father to them, and they became truly equal in his presence."*[89]

And Ibn Abbas رضي الله عنه said, *"The Prophet ﷺ was the most generous of all the people, and he ﷺ*

[88] Muslim, Sahih Muslim, Hadith 5726
[89] Ash-Shama'il Al-Muhammadiyah 335

used to become more generous in Ramadan when Gabriel met him. Gabriel used to meet him ﷺ every night during Ramadan to revise the Qur'an with him ﷺ. Allah's Messenger ﷺ then used to be more generous than the fast wind."[90]

Even when he ﷺ would be given something, he'd ask ﷺ whether that was a gift, or given in charity. If it were given as a gift, he'd keep it ﷺ and share it with those around him ﷺ if possible. But if the offering were meant as charity for him ﷺ, then he ﷺ would fully distribute it amongst the people. Abu Huraira رضي الله عنه said, *"Whenever a meal was brought to Allah's Messenger ﷺ, he would ask whether it was a gift or Sadaqa (something given in charity). If he ﷺ was told that it was Sadaqa, he ﷺ would tell his companions to eat it, but if it was a gift, he ﷺ would hurry to share it with them."[91]*

---

[90] Sahih al-Bukhari 3554 - Book 61, Hadith 63
[91] Sahih al-Bukhari 2576 - Book 51, Hadith 11

Science Behind Selflessness:

In today's fast-paced world, the significance of selflessness tends to go unnoticed by many. However, as a man seeking personal growth, it's crucial to understand the scientific basis behind this practice which Rasulullah ﷺ placed immense importance on — indicating a deeper purpose.

Fortunately, in our modern era, we are blessed with insights that reveal the multitude of health benefits associated with acts of generosity, impacting our mental and physical well-being. Many studies show that genuine acts of kindness, driven by pure goodness, can not only improve your health, but can also extend your lifespan.

According to Carolyn Gregoire, based on studies conducted by the University of Basel, *"Helping and supporting others may be key to living a longer and healthier life.*[92] Their conclusion was mainly sourced from both direct and indirect effects that being generous has on your neural and hormonal systems. According to the study, *"The neural and hormonal system that is activated in the process of caregiving represents a proximate mechanism that may reduce human mortality."*[93]

Seeking Help

Verily, in the name of the Most Merciful, we approach this topic with humility and grace. The guidance of our Prophet ﷺ shows us the path towards seeking aid and help. For in community and brotherhood, we find strength. And in supporting one another, true growth. The Quran teaches us the

---

[92] Carolyn Gregoire: Helping Others Is The Key To Longevity, Study Finds

[93] Sonja Hilbrand, David A. Coall, Denis Gerstorf, Ralph Hertwig: Caregiving within and beyond the family is associated with lower mortality for the caregiver

rewards for those who lend a hand to their brothers and sisters. However, what comes of those who seek the aid rather than give? What comes of those who constantly beg for help from all in matters big and small? In this subchapter, let us ponder and reflect on the beauty and wisdom of portraying independence in society.

First and foremost, as a Muslim, you must learn to depend on Allah for your needs, whether big or small. Rasulullah ﷺ said, *"Let one of you ask his Lord for his needs, all of them, even for a shoestring when his breaks."*[94] And then, after that, continue with your work, striving to fulfill your needs *independently*. Understanding that the one who begs others excessively can often face backlash is crucial. You never want to be known as that one person who is always seeking favors. Else, you will soon find yourself losing dignity in society.

---

[94] Sunan al-Tirmidhi 3973

Rasulullah ﷺ said, *"For one of you to take his rope and carry a bundle of wood to sell, by which Allah preserves his dignity, is better than begging from people who may give or withhold."*[95]

Seeking help too often can cause others to look down upon you, treat you with less respect, and distance themselves from you. Conversely, assuming even if they don't, and they give, subconsciously, they are placing themselves at a higher standing than you. And subconsciously, you will accept that exchange of power, essentially trading your self-respect for whatever you're seeking in that moment. And this is a subconscious fact that cannot be argued against. Rasulullah ﷺ said, *"The upper hand is better than the lower hand; the upper hand is that which gives and the lower hand is that which asks."*[96]

---

[95] Sahih al-Bukhari 1471
[96] Sunan an-Nasa'i 2533 - Book 23, Hadith 99

And the one who seeks independence from people, relying solely on Allah, will soon find Allah fulfilling all of his needs, InSha'Allah. Rasulullah ﷺ said, *"Whoever would abstain from asking people, Allah will make him abstinent. Whoever would be independent, Allah will make him independent. Whoever begs people while he owns an amount of five ounces of silver, he has asked importunately."*[97]

We learn from Abu Bakr رضي الله عنه that the Prophet ﷺ would personally advise him to avoid dependency. Ibn Abi Mulaykah said, *"Abu Bakr the truthful, may Allah be pleased with him, might drop the rein from his hand, so he would strike the leg of his camel to make it kneel and he would pick it up. They said to him, 'Why did you not order us to take care of it?' Abu Bakr said, 'My beloved Messenger*

---

[97] Musnad Ahmad 17237

of Allah, peace and blessings be upon him, commanded me not to ask people for anything."[98]

Nowadays, it seems that many are habitually leaning on one another, while living in a society where independence can easily be attained through the use of modern technology. Compare your issues with those during the Prophet's time ﷺ. You struggle with petty matters in life, while the sahaba struggled with poverty, hunger, lack of protection, abuse, etc. Yet they remained independent to the best of their ability. The Prophet of Allah ﷺ said, *"Whoever asks from people, while he is self-sufficient, only increases his share of the embers of Hellfire. They said, 'O Messenger of Allah, what amount of independence does not justify begging?' The Prophet said, 'Enough to eat in the morning and evening.'"*[99]

---

[98] Musnad Ahmad 65
[99] Sunan Abi Dawud 1629

❖ Understand: Seeking help is not always a bad thing. Depending on how often you seek it from people, and what sort of help you seek can actually portray you as someone of respect. For instance, seeking guidance from those more knowledgeable than you is good. Else how will you effectively learn and grow? Or including those around you in your decision-making will give them a sense of importance. And sometimes, if you're a man admired by many, having someone complete certain tasks for you will make them feel valued.

It's crucial to understand that while you should try your best to uphold independence in worldly matters, seeking help on matters that will make society better, or will improve your Hereafter is recommended. And seeking advice from those around you is from the sunnah of Rasulullah ﷺ as well. Even though he ﷺ was a Prophet of Allah, he ﷺ would still seek the advice of his companions ﷺ. For instance, during the treaty of Al-Hudaibiyah, the Prophet ﷺ consulted with his companions as to how they would approach the awaiting danger. The story is as follows.

The Prophet ﷺ and his companions were headed to Mecca for pilgrimage, due to which they were lightly armed with the sheathed swords of travelers only for protection. So on the way to Mecca, they reached a place known as Dhul-Hulaifah, where the Prophet ﷺ sent a companion to scout for news of the enemy. He eventually came back to tell the Prophet ﷺ that there was a large group of people blocking the roads to Mecca, waiting to oppose him ﷺ.

In this situation, although the Prophet ﷺ could have decided on his course of action ﷺ independently, he ﷺ sought the advice of his companions ﷺ, who were of the opinion that they should not fight unless they were stopped from performing their pilgrimage.[100]

So understand that following the prophetic orders of independence does not entail completely isolating yourself. It just means that you refrain from seeking excessive help, work to complete tasks on your own, and seek help either when it is absolutely needed, or when seeking help falls under acceptable forms of aid.

Now, how about when good comes to you from people without you seeking it? How should you respond? Should you accept their gifts, or should you display independence and rejection even then? We find the answers in the story of Umar ibn Al-Khattab رضي الله عنه.

Umar ibn Al-Khattab رضي الله عنه once made the mistake of falling into the extreme of Rasulullah's advice ﷺ on independence. Not only would Umar

---

[100] Safi-ur-Rahman Al-Mubarakpuri: Ar-Raheeq Al-Makhtum The Sealed Nectar, Pg.399

رضي الله عنه refrain from seeking his needs from the people, but he would also reject help when it came to him. Once when Rasulullah ﷺ had sent him a gift, Umar ibn Al-Khattab رضي الله عنه, out of love for Rasulullah's advice ﷺ, rejected the gift. This caused Rasulullah ﷺ to call him over and correct his mistake. The story is narrated by Imam Malik رضي الله عنه.

Imam Malik رضي الله عنه reported, *"Once the Messenger of Allah ﷺ sent a gift to Umar ibn al-Khattab رضي الله عنه, and Umar returned it. The Messenger of Allah ﷺ asked, 'Why did you return it?' He replied, 'Messenger of Allah, did you not tell us that it is better for us not to take anything from anyone?' The Messenger of Allah ﷺ said, 'That is by asking. Provision which Allah gives you is not the same as asking.' Umar ibn al-Khattab said, 'By the One in whose hand my self is, I will not ask anything from anyone, and anything that comes to me without my asking for it, I will accept.'"*[101]

❖ Understand: Asking is not the same as receiving. Exchanging and accepting gifts is from the sunnah, and is crucial for the betterment of society as a whole. According to Amy Novotney, *"Gift-giving activates regions of the brain associated with pleasure, social connection, and trust, creating a 'warm glow' effect."*[102]

By exploring the wisdom of Umar ibn Al-Khattab رضي الله عنه, and the teachings of Rasulullah ﷺ, you'll find a connection between acts of selflessness and the divine rewards that await you, both in this world and the Hereafter. However, now that you've learned the consequences of asking, it's also crucial

---

[101] Tafsir al-Qurtubi, Vol. 3 p.101
[102] Amy Novotney: What happens in your brain when you give a gift?

to understand what rewards await you for giving, especially to the needy.

And the answer is quite simple. Yes, Allah will reward you immensely for helping people out of their difficulties. Although, diving deeper, Allah will also reflect your help back at you at exponential levels. But how and why though? Because when you relieve your brother from hardship, Allah will take it upon Himself to relieve you from your difficulties.

Rasulullah ﷺ said, *"If anyone relieves a Muslim believer from one of the hardships of this worldly life, Allah will relieve him of one of the hardships of the Day of Resurrection. If anyone makes it easy for the one who is indebted to him (while finding it difficult to repay), Allah will make it easy for him in this worldly life and in the Hereafter, and if anyone conceals the faults of a Muslim, Allah will conceal his faults in this world and in the Hereafter. **Allah*** *helps His slave as long as he helps his brother.*"[103]

Stoicism

The notion of stoicism often carries the misconception that a man must remain serious and devoid of emotion at all times. However, this belief is not entirely accurate. Stoicism, in its essence, entails enduring pain and hardships without complaint while exemplifying wisdom, justice, and courage — though its interpretation has expanded over time. Originating around 300 B.C.E and later embraced by the Romans, this concept aligns closely with the core definition of a true man in Islam, as exemplified by the character of the Chosen One ﷺ.

---

[103] Related by Muslim - Book 16, Hadith 29

No individuals faced greater tribulations and challenges than the Messengers of Allah (peace be upon them all), and our beloved Prophet Muhammad ﷺ stands at the pinnacle of this fortitude. The Prophet ﷺ said, "*The most severely tested are the prophets and then the righteous. One of them would be tested with poverty until he could find nothing to cover himself but a cloak.*"[104]

❖ Understand: Tests and trials are from Allah. Allah's tests you encounter are not punishments, but rather indications of Allah's love for you. These tests are purposefully designed to elevate your status, fortify your position in society, and impart valuable lessons that facilitate your personal growth leading to self-improvement.

---

[104] Sunan Ibn Mājah 4024

❖ Note: It's crucial that you avoid complaining about trials, tribulations, and struggles to anyone but Allah. And it's also crucial to avoid overthinking alternative scenarios. Developing that 'what if' mentality will undoubtedly attract Shaytaan to your heart — not something you want when times are already difficult.

Rasulullah ﷺ said, *"If something befalls you, then do not say: If only I had done something else. Rather say: Allah has decreed what he wills. Verily, the phrase 'if only' opens the way for the work of Satan."*[105] Commenting on this hadith, Imam An-Nawawi said, *"'It opens the way for the work of Satan' means he casts into the heart opposition to the divine decree and Satan tempts him with it."*[106]

Utbah Ibn Ghazwan رضي الله عنه, a well-known companion of Rasulullah ﷺ, and one of the foremost military commanders of the Muslims, spoke about

---

[105] Sahih Muslim 2664
[106] Sharh Sahih Muslim 2664

his struggles that pushed his development as a powerful leader. Utbah رضي الله عنه would attribute the struggles and tests he went through from Allah to his success as a powerful leader.

He said, *"I was the seventh of seven people (to accept Islam) with the Messenger of Allah ﷺ. We had no food except for the leaves on trees that caused sores to develop around our mouths. I discovered a mantle and took it, splitting it between myself and Sa'd ibn Malik. There is none from the seven of us except that he is now the leader of a city — and you will experience first-hand the rulers after us!"*[107]

❖ Understand: These companions endured countless struggles, forging their leadership and manhood through unwavering virtue and resilience. Yet, theirs and all others' feats pale in comparison to the challenges faced by Rasulullah ﷺ. From a tender age,

---

[107] Al-Tirmidhi, Al-Shama'il al-Muhammadiyyah, Hadith 374

he ﷺ experienced the sorrow of being an orphan and toiling as a shepherd. Then, upon attaining prophethood, he ﷺ endured persecution and torture, followed by the losses of beloved family members. Insults, humiliation, and even stoning became part of his journey ﷺ. And if that physical and mental burden wasn't heavy enough, he ﷺ lived on to bury multiple of his children throughout his lifetime ﷺ.

However, despite the relentless trials from Allah, our Prophet ﷺ ensured that his face ﷺ radiated nothing but a smile, with his presence welcoming, with his heart loving, and with his emotions never negative. Considering the multitude and weight of the burdens he ﷺ faced, one might expect him ﷺ to have displayed constant irritation, anger, and despair. Yet, on the contrary, his unwavering manhood ﷺ sets an awe-inspiring example for all men to follow.

Jabir رضي الله عنه talks about the day the Muslims dug a trench around Medina to keep the invaders away. He says, *"We were digging (the trench) on the day of (the Trench) and we came across a big solid rock. We went to the Prophet ﷺ and said, 'Here is a rock appearing across the trench.' He ﷺ said, 'I am coming down.' Then he got up, and a stone was tied to his belly for we had not eaten anything for three days."*[108]

❖ Understand: Working tirelessly, just as hard as his companions ﷺ, while devoid of food, with a war quickly approaching, the Prophet ﷺ still maintained a soft and calm attitude. He ﷺ didn't yell nor blame others. Nor did he ﷺ complain about his situation ﷺ to the people, because true strength shines brightest when pressure is applied. He ﷺ said, *"The strong are*

---

[108] Sahih al-Bukhari 4101 - Book 64, Hadith 145

not the best wrestlers. Verily, the strong are only those who control themselves when they are angry."[109]

And particularly when you possess the means to unleash your emotions, yet exercise restraint over them, Rasulullah ﷺ said that Allah will bless you with immense rewards. He ﷺ said, *"Whoever controls his anger at the time when he has the means to act upon it, Allah will fill his heart with contentment on the Day of Resurrection."*[110]

You will find peace, gratitude, and inner fulfillment when blessed with contentment. In this Dunya, that contentment will allow you to appreciate the present moment, embrace simplicity, and find joy in the smallest of things. But on the Day of Judgment, that contentment will serve as one of the most sought blessings from Allah.

---

[109] Sahih al-Bukhari 6114, Sahih Muslim 2609
[110] Reported by al-Tabarani, 12/453, Sahih al-Jami 6518

Justice

Justice stands as a vital pillar of stoicism, for it serves as the backbone that upholds and ties together many other principles. In order for a man to amass respect and honor in society, he must be fair, for embracing justice will allow him to maintain harmony within himself and his interactions with others. Thus constituting a balanced and virtuous life. Allah explicitly commands us in the Quran to embody justice, regardless of who that justice will stand against. He says:

يَا أَيُّهَا الَّذِينَ آمَنُواْ كُونُواْ قَوَّامِينَ بِالْقِسْطِ شُهَدَاء لِلَّهِ وَلَوْ عَلَى أَنفُسِكُمْ أَوِ الْوَالِدَيْنِ وَالأَقْرَبِينَ إِن يَكُنْ غَنِيًّا أَوْ فَقَيرًا فَاللّهُ أَوْلَى بِهِمَا فَلاَ تَتَّبِعُواْ الْهَوَى أَن تَعْدِلُواْ وَإِن تَلْوُواْ أَوْ تُعْرِضُواْ فَإِنَّ اللّهَ كَانَ بِمَا تَعْمَلُونَ خَبِيرًا ﴿١٣٥﴾

O you who have believed, be persistently standing firm in justice, witnesses for Allah, even if it be against yourselves or parents and relatives. Whether one is rich or poor, Allah is more worthy

of both. So follow not [personal] inclination, lest
you not be just. And if you distort [your testimony]
or refuse [to give it], then indeed Allah is ever, of
what you do, Aware.
(Quran 4:135)

Looking back at the origins of stoicism, we see that
the stoics divided justice into a few themes. These
themes included piety, honesty, equity, and fair
dealing. Or in other words, many ideas from
stoicism align with the teachings of Rasulullah ﷺ.
From his teachings ﷺ, when Imam Ali رضي الله عنه
was asked about justice, he said, *"Justice is putting*
things in their proper places while generosity is
extracting them away from their [original]
destinations."[111] Allah says in the Quran:

---

[111] Al-Qashani, Adab al-Tariqah wa Asrar al-Haqiqah, p.33,
Dawud Walid: Futuwwah

إِنَّ اللَّهَ يَأْمُرُكُمْ أَن تُؤَدُّواْ الأَمَانَاتِ إِلَى أَهْلِهَا وَإِذَا حَكَمْتُم بَيْنَ النَّاسِ أَن

تَحْكُمُواْ بِالْعَدْلِ

Surely, Allah commands you to deliver trusts to those entitled to them, and that, when you judge between people, judge with justice.

(Quran 4:58)

To look at a group of people and be able to call them hypocrites and wrongdoers without a doubt is indeed a disgraceful presence. And when we look at the pre-Islamic society of the Arabs, more specifically the Quraish and the Meccans, it's challenging to picture that any good could have come from them. Especially considering that a few of their standard practices were to bury their daughters, ill-treat the poor, humiliate the women, display their tyranny and Jahiliya over the weak, steal from the poor, and so much more.

Yet, we know that to these people was born the greatest of Allah's Creation ﷺ. The Creation who the people titled, *"al-Sadiq (The Truthful)"* and *"al-Amin (The Trustworthy)."* He ﷺ would go on to defy their misguided definition of manhood and set the foundation for true masculinity by inspiring man to uphold honesty. Because honesty is a key characteristic of justice. Imam Ali ibn Abi Talib رضي الله عنه said, *"The truthfulness of a man is based upon the measure of his manhood."*[112]

❖ Note: The concept of justice lives on a multitude of levels ranging from petty everyday matters, to life and death situations. You, as a young man, will most likely not find yourself having to make decisions against your family in severe matters. Rather, if you're in school, your justice may be tested during feuds and discord between friends. Or if you're in the corporate or business space, your justice may be tested during dishonest/immoral dealings, office politics, etc.

---

[112] Al-Tamimi, Ghurar al-Hikam wa Durar al-Kalim, p.174

The point is, whatever your situation, upholding proper morals is vital for your manhood. Rasulullah ﷺ said, *"There is a Sadaqa to be given for every joint of the human body; and for every day on which the sun rises there is a reward of a Sadaqa (i.e. charitable gift) for the one who establishes justice among people."*[113]

Wisdom

Wisdom encompasses the very essence of a man, defining his demeanor, emotions, and, most importantly, life experiences. Unlike other qualities, wisdom is not easily acquired through conscious pursuit. It emerges from the depths of a man's journey, forged through struggles and tribulations. It belongs to those who have experienced life's lower, darker side and have gleaned invaluable lessons.

Using the lessons they've learned through such experiences, they are then able to navigate future

---

[113] Sahih al-Bukhari 2707 - Book 53, Hadith 17

challenges better, enlightening their path. And those people who are blessed with such wisdom, are also able to illuminate a path for those who seek their guidance. These are the people who Allah has blessed, for they are able to use their knowledge for the betterment of others. And thus, it is essential to recognize that Allah bestows wisdom upon those He wills, parallel to Allah testing those He loves. Allah says in the Quran:

$$يُؤْتِي الْحِكْمَةَ مَن يَشَاء وَمَن يُؤْتَ الْحِكْمَةَ فَقَدْ أُوتِيَ خَيْرًا كَثِيرًا وَمَا يَذَّكَّرُ إِلاَّ أُوْلُواْ الأَلْبَابِ ﴿٢٦٩﴾$$

Allah grants wisdom to whoever He wills. And whoever is granted wisdom is certainly blessed with a great privilege. But none will be mindful [of this] except people of reason.
(Quran 2:269)

Now turning our focus toward the life of Rasulullah ﷺ, we discover illustrations of his profound wisdom

ﷺ in pursuit of his ultimate mission of spreading Islam. A testament to his wisdom ﷺ unfolds during the story of Ta'if, a city that holds significance in his life ﷺ. It was Ta'if where the Prophet ﷺ, accompanied by his adopted son Zaid bin Haritha رضي الله عنه, sought to convey the message of Islam after being compelled to flee Mecca. And it was in Ta'if that he ﷺ faced rejection. And it was in Ta'if where Rasulullah ﷺ faced one of the hardest days of his life ﷺ.

When he ﷺ approached the three leaders of Ta'if, attempting to convince them of Islam, they insulted and mocked him ﷺ. The first of the three said, *"He is tearing the cloths of the Kaaba; is it true that Allah has sent you as a messenger?"* The second one replied to our Prophet ﷺ, stating, *"Has Allah not found someone else to entrust him with His message?"* Finally, the last one mocked, *"I swear by Allah that I will never speak to you. If you really are the Messenger of Allah, then you are too important to be speaking to me. If you are lying against Allah, then I should never speak to you."* Understanding that these people were hopeless cases, our Prophet ﷺ left them saying, *"Since you are behaving this way, please do not disclose my presence here."[114]*

Following this, the Prophet ﷺ spent approximately another ten days in the city. However, after these ten days, the Prophet ﷺ quickly faced an unfortunate turn of events. Provoked by their leaders, the people of Ta'if began chasing him ﷺ out of the city with a barrage of stones.

The misguided people, accompanied by their servants, jeered and taunted the Prophet ﷺ through the narrow streets and alleyways of Ta'if. Their relentless assault caused him ﷺ to flee the city, running through the scorching desert with both his legs ﷺ drenched in blood.

---

[114] Safi-ur-Rahman Al-Mubarakpuri: Ar-Raheeq Al-Makhtum The Sealed Nectar, Pg.162

In one narration, the Prophet's wife ﷺ, Aisha رضي الله عنها asked him ﷺ, *"Have you ever experienced a worse day than Uhud?"* He ﷺ answered, *"Your tribes have troubled me very much, and the **worst was the day of Aqaba** when I presented myself to Ibn Abd Yalail ibn Abd Kulal and he did not respond to what I intended. I departed, overwhelmed with excessive sorrow, and I could not relax until I found myself at a tree where I lifted my head towards the sky to see a cloud shading me.*

I looked up and saw Gabriel in it. He called me saying: 'Allah has heard your people's saying to you and how they have replied, and Allah has sent the Angel of the Mountains to you that you may order him to do whatever you wish to these people.' The Angel of the Mountains greeted me and he said: 'O Muhammad, order what you wish, and if you like, I will let the mountains fall on them.' The Prophet ﷺ said, 'No, rather I hope that Allah will bring from their descendants people who will worship Allah alone without associating partners with Him.'"[115]

❖ Note: In this testament to the mercy and wisdom of our Prophet ﷺ, and the Will of Allah, Ta'if stands today as a thriving city with a Muslim majority population. You witness thousands of devoted Muslims worshiping Allah on the same grounds where their ancestors once pelted the Prophet ﷺ with stones. Had he ﷺ wished, the angel of the mountains would've crushed its inhabitants. But rather, the Prophet's long-term vision ﷺ and his mercy ﷺ exemplify his wisdom ﷺ. He ﷺ prioritized patience over immediate revenge and vengeance.

---

[115] Book 59, Hadith 42 - Book 59, Hadith 42

Courage & Determination

The longing to fit in, the weight of oppression, and the temptation to follow misguided paths can feel like formidable locks holding you back. You're afraid to break free from them, because if you do, how will the world then perceive you? What will society think of you? To learn effective navigation through such waters, you must start by embodying courage. For it is through the essence of courage, as exemplified by the Chosen One ﷺ, that you not only will possess the ability to break free from these constraints, but also the strength to tackle the potential backlash from society.

Following his sunnah ﷺ, can you learn what it means for a man to truly embody courage in his character. Because, how can you as a man not follow in the footsteps of your Leader ﷺ, who stood as courageous as anyone around him? Anas ibn

Malik رضي الله عنه said, *"The Messenger of Allah ﷺ was the most courageous of men"*[116]

And Abu Sa'id al-Khudri رضي الله عنه reported that the Prophet ﷺ said, *"Let not fear of the people prevent one of you from speaking the truth, if he knows it."*[117] And you'll find that when you stand firm in your values, eventually, even those who stand against you may begin to respect you. Allah says in the Quran:

$$وَلَا تَسْتَوِي الْحَسَنَةُ وَلَا السَّيِّئَةُ ادْفَعْ بِالَّتِي هِيَ أَحْسَنُ فَإِذَا الَّذِي بَيْنَكَ وَبَيْنَهُ عَدَاوَةٌ كَأَنَّهُ وَلِيٌّ حَمِيمٌ ﴿٣٤﴾$$

And not equal are the good deed and the bad. Repel [evil] by that [deed] which is better; and thereupon, the one whom between you and him is enmity [will become] as though he was a devoted friend.

(Quran 41:34)

---

[116] Al-Bukhari, Sahih Al-Bukhari, Hadith 6033; Muslim, Sahih Muslim, Hadith 2307
[117] Musnad Ahmad 11459

Fear of Isolation

When the Prophet ﷺ began preaching Islam, the Pagans despised it. They demonstrated much opposition and hatred towards both the Prophet ﷺ and his message ﷺ. Eventually, their pressure had mounted to such an extent that they began to target the Prophet's uncle, Abu Talib, a Meccan chief. Although he wasn't a Muslim, he still loved and supported his nephew ﷺ.

The Pagans demanded that he convince the Prophet ﷺ to give up on Islam. They warned Abu Talib of the consequences his nephew ﷺ would face if he ﷺ continued. Now, deeply concerned for the well-being of the Prophet ﷺ, Abu Talib approached Rasulullah ﷺ and shared the Pagans' demands, seeking a resolution for this challenging situation. Abu Talib said to Rasulullah ﷺ, *"Spare me and yourself and put not burden on me that I can't bear."*

Remember that the Prophet ﷺ had little to no support at this point. Most of his followers ﷺ were from amongst the slaves of Mecca and the lower class. One of his only significant supporters ﷺ at this time was his uncle, Abu Talib.

So upon hearing his uncle's words, he ﷺ thought that his uncle would abandon him ﷺ, leaving him ﷺ with little to no worldly support. Yet, trusting that Allah would stand by his side ﷺ, the Prophet ﷺ responded, *"O my uncle! By Allah if they put the sun in my right hand and the moon in my left on condition that I abandon this course, I would not abandon it until Allah has made me victorious or I perish therein."*

Then as the prophet ﷺ was getting up to leave, Abu Talib called him ﷺ back and said, *"Go and preach what you please, for by Allah, I will never forsake you."*[118]

---

[118] Safi-ur-Rahman Al-Mubarakpuri: Ar-Raheeq Al-Makhtum The Sealed Nectar: Ibn Hisham 1/265, 266, and Dala'il An-Nubuwwah by Al-Baihaqi, 2/188

❖ Understand: This city, Mecca, was the birthplace of Rasulullah ﷺ. These people, the Quraish, were his people ﷺ. And this uncle, Abu Talib, was the man who raised him ﷺ after his parents and grandfather had passed away ﷺ. So for him ﷺ to not only stand against his entire city, but also against the man who was like a father to him ﷺ for the sake of Allah, must've required an immense amount of courage and determination. This is what highlights a man's character. A man is he who will go to lengths for the truth, for what he believes in. Not someone who will drift wherever the wind takes him. Malcolm X once said, *'A man who stands for nothing will fall for anything.'*

Appearance

In the pursuit of personal growth, it is ideal for a man to cultivate an appealing appearance, a task that holds much significance in Islam, yet is often overlooked. The Prophet ﷺ said, *"Verily, Allah is beautiful and He loves beauty."*[119]

However, a man must understand that attractiveness encompasses more than just facial features. Rather, beauty includes the entirety of one's body and demeanor. Only by harnessing both aspects of beauty, physical and internal, can a man truly be considered attractive. Although, this subchapter will focus specifically on developing a positive external appearance.

It is essential to remember that you are a Creation of Allah, the ultimate Creator who fashioned you with care and precision. Your physical attributes and characteristics are crafted in His image. Therefore, it is unsuitable for you to criticize your perceived flaws or imperfections. Allah says in the Quran:

---

[119] al-Mu'jam al-Awsat 6906

لَقَدْ خَلَقْنَا الْإِنسَانَ فِي أَحْسَنِ تَقْوِيمٍ ﴿٤﴾

Indeed, We created humans in the best form.

(Quran 95:4)

However, this does not mean you don't try to build upon your inherent beauty. Instead of despairing over your physical flaws, as a man, your focus must be on embracing and utilizing your inherent qualities to their full extent. Like a skilled strategist, you must strive to master every card in your deck, harnessing and cultivating your strengths to be the best version of yourself. Because as cited by numerous studies, men who keep their physical appearance in check tend to attract more respect and influence in society than men who don't. This may be a sad reality, but according to Amy Gallo, *"When an employee looks unkempt… they may have a harder time gaining their colleagues' or customers' respect."*[120]

---

[120] Amy Gallo: How to Give an Employee Feedback About Their Appearance

So what does it mean to appear 'kept'? How can you appear better to impress those around you? In this subchapter, *His Appearance,* you will learn the masculine character exemplified by our Rasool ﷺ, focusing particularly on the ideal, external aspects that define a man.

This subchapter will shed light on his dietary practices ﷺ, prophetic routines for building physical strength, practical and spiritual methods for radiating a natural glow, and cultivating an overall appealing appearance. By incorporating these principles into your lives, not only can you strive to better yourselves, but you'll also be able to lead a life with a more eye-catching, external appearance.

Diet

وكُلُواْ وَاشْرَبُواْ وَلاَ تُسْرِفُواْ إِنَّهُ لاَ يُحِبُّ الْمُسْرِفِينَ ﴿٣١﴾

and eat and drink, but be not excessive. Indeed, He
likes not those who commit excess.
(Quran 7:31)

Diet remains one of the more critical aspects of appearance as it constitutes for much of the body's health and facial appearance. Our Prophet ﷺ said, *"A human being fills no worse vessel than his stomach. It is sufficient for a human being to eat a few mouthfuls to keep his spine straight (to stay healthy). But if he must (fill it), then one third of food, one third for drink and one third for air."*[121]

The food you consume and how you nourish your body carries a significant impact on various aspects of your health. It goes beyond simply satisfying hunger. What you choose to consume and

---

[121] Sunan Ibn Majah - Book 29, Hadith 99

the quantity at which you consume your food can directly influence your facial appearance and overall physicality. For instance, there is no doubt that acne causes your face to look worse than it would without it. And the food you consume plays a significant role in the regulation of acne. According to Erica Julson, MS, RDN, *"Acne is strongly associated with eating a Western-style diet rich in calories, fat and refined carbohydrates."*[122]

Notice how Erica mentioned foods that are usually very filling and overall not ideal for your body. And while consuming excessive amounts of such food can lead to a negative appearance, it can also make you lazy — not the ideal state a man would want to find himself in. According to Lauren Harris-Pincus, M.S., RDN, *"Eating beyond your point of satisfaction can also cause a sense of drowsiness or feeling sluggish as the body is redirecting its attention to digesting the excess*

---

[122] Erica Julson: Healthline

food."[123] This is a strong reason why you may feel more productive during Ramadan while fasting, even though your body is deprived of energy.

Now what does research say about the decline in cognitive performance? How are your cognitive skills impacted based on your food consumption? Lianna Bass cites a 2009 study on obesity and cognition by Erik Nilsson. She says, *"A 2009 study linked obesity to mental decline in older folks, even when controlling for obesity-related diseases. So, having obesity may also reduce cognitive abilities like memory."*[124]

❖ Understand: A valuable lesson to glean from this is that treating your body with fairness involves mindful eating habits. Acting on impulsive urges and overindulging can be unfair to your body and overall

---

[123] Lainey Younkin, M.S., RD, LDN
[124] Overweight and cognition, Lianna Bass

mental health. Rather, it will prove beneficial for you to practice moderation and portion control. Our Prophet ﷺ said, *"A believer eats in one intestine (is satisfied with a little food), and a kafir (unbeliever) or a hypocrite eats in seven intestines (eats too much)."*[125]

However, to achieve a balanced and healthy lifestyle, avoiding extremes and finding a middle ground regarding your eating habits is crucial. Overeating is never a sustainable or beneficial approach to life, but neither is starving yourself. Whether you are restricting your food intake drastically to lose weight rapidly, or incorrectly adhering to Islamic guidelines out of religious devotion, it's important to recognize that depriving your body of essential nutrients can adversely affect your overall well-being.

Rasulullah ﷺ taught us to live in moderation. Sleep moderately, enjoy moderately, worship

---

[125] Sahih al-Bukhari 5394 - Book 70, Hadith 22

moderately, and eat moderately, for he ﷺ looked down upon extremism. The Prophet ﷺ said, *"And beware of going to extremes in religious matters, for those who came before you were destroyed because of going to extremes in religious matters."*[126]

And nowadays, you may see 'religious' figures who grow an unkept physique. However, that is not what Islam teaches you. Just as you worship moderately, you must eat moderately to stay in shape as well. Once Umar ibn al-Khattab رضي الله عنه saw a man with a large belly, to which Umar asked, *"'What is this?' The man said, 'It is a blessing from Allah.' Umar said, 'No, rather it is a punishment.'"*[127]

Rasulullah ﷺ also said that the one who eats to his full in this world would be the hungriest on the Day of Resurrection. He ﷺ said, *"Restrain your belching,*

---

[126] Sunan an-Nasa'i 3057 - Book 24, Hadith 440
[127] Hadith Muhammad ibn Abd Allah al-Ansari 42

for those who were most satiated in the world will be the most hungry on the Day of Resurrection."[128] And as a testament to this, the wife of Rasulullah ﷺ, Aisha رضي الله عنها said, *"The family of Muhammad, peace and blessings be upon him, never ate to their fill of wheat bread for three consecutive nights, ever since they had come to Medina, until he passed away."*[129]

Prophetic Foods

As you strive to embody the noble qualities of the Chosen One ﷺ, it's important that you also add his dietary preferences ﷺ to your arsenal. In this subsection, you will learn what he ﷺ found most pleasing on his plate ﷺ as mentioned in hadith. Provided for you is a list of a few common foods that the prophet ﷺ would enjoy:

---

[128] Sunan al-Tirmidhi 2478
[129] Sahih al-Bukhari 6089, Sahih Muslim 2970

- **Barley:** Anas bin Malik رضي الله عنه said, *"A tailor invited Allah's Messenger ﷺ to a meal which he had prepared. I went with Allah's Messenger ﷺ to that meal, and the tailor served the Prophet ﷺ with barley bread and soup of gourd and cured meat."*[130]

- **Dates:** The Messenger of Allah ﷺ said, *"When one of you breaks his fast, then let him do so with dried dates, for they are blessed. Whoever does not find dates, then water, for it is purifying."*[131]

- **Olive Oil:** The Prophet of Allah ﷺ said, *"Season (your food) with olive oil and anoint yourselves with it, for it comes from a blessed tree."*[132]

---

[130] Sahih al-Bukhari 5439 - Book 70, Hadith 67
[131] Jami at-Tirmidhi 658 - Book 7, Hadith 42
[132] Sunan Ibn Majah 3319 - Book 29, Hadith 69

167

- **Honey:** Aisha رضي الله عنها said, *"The Messenger of Allah, peace and blessings be upon him, used to like sweets and honey."*[133] And apart from simply liking honey, the Prophet ﷺ also noted honey as one of the best cures for us. He ﷺ said, *"You must make use of two healers: the Quran and honey."*[134]

- **Pumpkin:** Anas رضي الله عنه said, *"A tailor invited the Prophet to a meal which he had prepared and I went along with the Prophet. He presented barley bread and soup containing pumpkin and dried sliced meat, and I saw the Prophet going after the pumpkin round the dish, so I have always liked pumpkin since that day."*[135]

- **Milk:** Rasulullah ﷺ said that there is good in drinking milk. He ﷺ said, *"Verily, Allah Almighty*

---

[133] Sahih al-Bukhari 5115
[134] Shu'ab al-Iman 2345
[135] Mishkat al-Masabih 4180

did not place an ailment but that he also placed its cure. You should drink the milk of cows, for they are given health by all kinds of plants."[136]

- **Melons:** Aisha رضي الله عنها said, "The Messenger of Allah ﷺ used to eat melon with fresh dates, and he used to say: The heat of the one is broken by the coolness of the other, and the coolness of the one by the heat of the other."[137]

- **Grapes:** Ibn Umar رضي الله عنه said, "In our holy battles, we used to get honey and grapes, as war booty which we would eat and would not store."[138]

Fitness

It is crucial for a man to reflect on the actions and habits of his role models. When observing elders,

---

[136] Musnad Ahmad 18352
[137] Sunan Abi Dawud 3836 - Book 28, Hadith 101
[138] Sahih al-Bukhari 3154 - Book 57, Hadith 62

you may find different patterns of behavior. Some spend their time in the mosques, engaging in worship, which is commendable. Others, however, seem to pass their days without purpose, devoid of productivity. As a man, a follower of Rasulullah ﷺ, you cannot afford to look weak. You are young, yet when the Prophet ﷺ received his prophethood ﷺ, he was at the age of forty.

Studying his life ﷺ, we find that he and his companions ﷺ remained active, vibrant, and even surpassed the youth of their time. For example, they fought in tedious battles where the opposing armies heavily outnumbered them. And while you understand that Rasulullah's eating habits ﷺ were one of the key factors that kept him ﷺ healthy even at an old age, there were other elements to it as well — elements such as fitness.

In this section of *Appearance*, you will learn of the more physical habits of our Prophet ﷺ that not only contributed to his overall physical health ﷺ, but also allowed him ﷺ to stay steadfast upon his mission ﷺ even through old age.

The Powerful Man

Oftentimes, when you look at men in positions of leadership, you'll find that the most appealing of them are those who are physically attractive. Perhaps it's their facial radiance, their striking looks, or in many cases, their well-trained, masculine physique. As a man, it's your responsibility to stay in shape in order to not only portray a positive demeanor, but also stay physically strong. Because a strong man can protect not only himself, but also those around him. Therefore, Rasulullah ﷺ said, *"The strong believer is more beloved to Allah than the weak believer, but there is goodness in both of them."*[139] And the Prophet ﷺ was amongst the strongest of men as seen in the story of Rukhana.

---

[139] Sahih Muslim 2664

Once, a man named Rukhana, who was a well-known wrestler, challenged the Prophet ﷺ to a wrestling match, overconfident in his abilities. Undeterred by him, the Prophet ﷺ gracefully accepted his challenge. However, in no way would Rukhana expect to witness firsthand just how powerful the Prophet ﷺ was.

The Prophet ﷺ effortlessly pinned Rukhana to the ground multiple times, back-to-back, before Rukhana could even comprehend how, leaving him in a state of awe and disbelief. Ali ibn Rukhana said, *"Rukanah wrestled with the Prophet ﷺ and the Prophet ﷺ threw him on the ground."*[140]

In another hadith on athletics, this time regarding archery, we find that the Prophet ﷺ highly encouraged practicing it. Salama bin Al-Akwa narrated, *"The Prophet ﷺ passed by some persons*

---

[140] Sunan Abi Dawud 4078 - Book 34, Hadith 59

of the tribe of Aslam practicing archery (i.e. the throwing of arrows). Allah's Messenger ﷺ said, 'O offspring of Ishmael! Practice archery (i.e. arrow throwing) as your father was a great archer (i.e. arrow-thrower).'"[141] He ﷺ also said, *"If anyone abandons archery after becoming an adept through distaste for it, it is a blessing he has abandoned; or he said: for which he has been ungrateful."*[142]

Developing a Prophetic Physique

Now, as for the importance of working out to build a positive demeanor, when people see you as a man who goes to the gym, trains, and cares about his masculinity, they will subconsciously associate respectable traits with you. For instance, you having developed arms, a wide back, a built chest, and legs complimenting the rest of your physique, portrays that you have the trait of consistency. Because you

---

[141] Sahih al-Bukhari 3373 - Book 60, Hadith 47
[142] Sunan Abi Dawud 2513 - Book 15, Hadith 37

don't just get an eye-striking physique by only training occasionally. It also tells people that you carry the traits of discipline, delayed gratification, and focus — all traits that are highly respected in a man, found in the masculinity of Rasulullah ﷺ.

Now, you may be wondering what exactly the Prophet ﷺ looked like. And how did his physique ﷺ equate to modern-day aesthetics? First and foremost, we know that the prophet ﷺ engaged in sports. He ﷺ said, *"Everything in which there is no remembrance of Allah is idle play, except four things: a man playing with his wife; a man training his horse; a man running between two lines (as in a race); and a man learning how to swim."*[143]

Yet apart from his athletics ﷺ, in the following list, you'll find certain muscle groups that stood out in the Prophet's physique ﷺ. Read through them, so

---

[143] Narrated by an-Nasaa'i in as-Sunan al-Kubra 8889, classed as saheeh by al-Albaani in as-Saheehah 315

that you know what to prioritize in your training at the gym to achieve that prophetic figure InSha'Allah.

- **Chest:** The Prophet ﷺ was known to have an attractive, wide chest. Al-Hasan ibn 'Ali رضي الله عنه said, *"He was well proportioned in physique, firmly cohesive, with the stomach and the breast in even balance. He was wide-chested..."*[144] Ibn Al-Abbas رضي الله عنه also says, *"His chest was broad and flatted."*[145]

- **Shoulders and Back:** According to numerous sources, Rasulullah ﷺ was known to have a broad upper body. Al-Bara رضي الله عنه narrated, *"He had hair that would flow on his shoulders, having broad shoulders..."*[146] And Ali bin Abi

---

[144] Ash-Shama'il Al-Muhammadiyah 8 - Book 1, Hadith 7
[145] Ar-Raheeq Al-Makhtum The Sealed Nectar, P.576 - Khulasatus-Siyar p.20
[146] Jami at-Tirmidhi 3635 - Book 49, Hadith 31

Talib رضي الله عنه said, *"His limbs and shoulder joints were rather big."*[147]

- **Legs:** The legs of the Prophet ﷺ were known to be powerful, allowing him ﷺ to walk significantly faster than the rest of his companions ﷺ. Ibn Al-Abbas رضي الله عنه, describing the legs of Rasulullah ﷺ, said, *"His legs were plain, straight, and stretched. His other limbs were also large."*[148]

  And Abu Huraira رضي الله عنه described how even the youngsters would struggle to keep pace with the Prophet ﷺ. He said, *"Nor have I seen anyone more **rapid** in his **gait** than Allah's Messenger (Allah bless him and give him peace). The earth seemed to be folded up for*

---

[147] Ar-Raheeq Al-Makhtum The Sealed Nectar, P.573 - Ibn Hisham 1/401, Jami At-Tirmidhi 4/303
[148] Ar-Raheeq Al-Makhtum The Sealed Nectar, P.576 - Khulasatus-Siyar p.20

him. We must strenuously exert ourselves, while he is not subject to any stress."[149]

- **Arms:** The Prophet ﷺ had well-developed arms. Ibn Al-Abbas رضي الله عنه said, *"He had long forearms with expansive palms."[150]*

- **Stomach:** Now unlike Rasulullah's other features ﷺ, his stomach ﷺ was neither large nor wide. Rather, he ﷺ kept it maintained well behind the line of his chest ﷺ. Umm Ma'bad Al-Khuza'iyah describing the Prophet ﷺ said, *"Neither was his belly bulging out nor was his head deprived of hair."[151]* And in another hadith, Abu At-Tufail رضي الله عنه, describing the body

---

[149] Ash-Shama'il Al-Muhammadiyah 122 - Book 18, Hadith 1
[150] Ar-Raheeq Al-Makhtum The Sealed Nectar, P.576 - Khulasatus-Siyar p.20
[151] Ar-Raheeq Al-Makhtum The Sealed Nectar, P.572 - Zadul-Ma'ad 2/45

composition of Rasulullah ﷺ, said, *"He was neither fat nor thin…"*[152]

Noor

Noor, derived from the Arabic language, translates to *light.* However, the significance of noor cannot be justified simply by its linguistic meaning. Noor represents a radiant splendor, an innate beauty coming from Allah. And noor is considered a divine light that Allah bestows upon whom He wills. Allah says in the Quran:

اللَّهُ نُورُ السَّمَاوَاتِ وَالْأَرْضِ مَثَلُ نُورِهِ كَمِشْكَاةٍ فِيهَا مِصْبَاحٌ الْمِصْبَاحُ فِي زُجَاجَةٍ الزُّجَاجَةُ كَأَنَّهَا كَوْكَبٌ دُرِّيٌّ يُوقَدُ مِن شَجَرَةٍ مُّبَارَكَةٍ زَيْتُونِةٍ لَّا شَرْقِيَّةٍ وَلَا غَرْبِيَّةٍ يَكَادُ زَيْتُهَا يُضِيءُ وَلَوْ لَمْ تَمْسَسْهُ نَارٌ نُّورٌ عَلَى نُورٍ يَهْدِي اللَّهُ لِنُورِهِ مَن يَشَاء وَيَضْرِبُ اللَّهُ الْأَمْثَالَ لِلنَّاسِ وَاللَّهُ بِكُلِّ شَيْءٍ عَلِيمٌ ﴿٣٥﴾

---

[152] Ar-Raheeq Al-Makhtum The Sealed Nectar, P.573

Allah is the Light of the heavens and the earth. His light is like a niche in which there is a lamp, the lamp is in a crystal, the crystal is like a shining star, lit from [the oil of] a blessed olive tree, [located] neither to the east nor the west, whose oil would almost glow, even without being touched by fire. Light upon light! Allah guides whoever He wills to His light. And Allah sets forth parables for humanity. For Allah has [perfect] knowledge of all things.
(Quran 24:35)

When beauty is mentioned, it is often centered around external appearance and ways to enhance it. However, in searching for ways to improve that external beauty, you may often overlook the connection between your inner beauty and its direct influence on your outer beauty.

Islam acknowledges and emphasizes the significance of both inner and outer magnificence, highlighting the concept of *noor* as a prime example. Noor, referring to divine light, is deeply affected by your actions and deeds. The more goodness you embody, the brighter your heart shines, illuminating your countenance. Conversely, indulging in sins casts a shadow over your heart, darkening them and negatively impacting your appearance.

However, repent if you've sinned and feel like your heart has darkened. Do not despair in the Mercy of Allah. Because only through seeking the Forgiveness of Allah after sinning, can you hope to replenish that lost divine light in your heart, consequently, on your face. Rasulullah ﷺ said, *"Verily, when the servant commits a sin, a black mark appears upon his heart. If he abandons the sin, seeks forgiveness, and repents, then his heart will be polished. If he returns to the sin, the blackness will be increased until it overcomes his heart."*[153] Then Imam Ali رضي الله عنه also gives a detailed explanation of noor.

---

[153] Sunan al-Tirmidhī 3334

He says, *"Verily, faith begins like a fragment of white in the heart. Each time faith increases in magnitude, it increases that brightness. When he completes his faith, the entire heart is brightened. Verily, hypocrisy begins like a fragment in the heart. Each time hypocrisy increases in magnitude, it increases that darkness. When he completes his hypocrisy, the entire heart is darkened. I swear by Allah, if you were to split open the heart of a believer, you would find brightness and if you were to split open the heart of a hypocrite, you would find darkness."*[154]

❖ Understand: While beauty and noor may intersect one another, it is crucial to remember that they are not the same. Beauty is skin-deep, based on physical factors such as your health, genetics, facial structure, etc. On the other hand, noor is a light from Allah that brightens your face by entering your heart. It can be

---

[154] Shu'ab al-Iman 37

attracted through good, such as your five daily salats, dhikr, Quran, dua, nafil, Tahajjud, etc. Rasulullah ﷺ said, *"Verily, good deeds bring brightness upon the face, a light in the heart, an expanse of provision, strength in the body, and love in the hearts of the creation. And evil deeds bring blackness upon the face, darkness in the grave and in the heart, weakness in the body, a restriction of provision, and hatred in the hearts of the creation."*[155]

Conversely, although noor and beauty are different aspects of your overall attractiveness, they still transit paths. One of their intersections is at trimming your mustaches and letting your beards grow. Rasulullah ﷺ said, *"Be different from the idolaters. Let the beard grow and trim the moustache."*[156]

---

[155] al-Jawab al-Kafi 1/54
[156] Sahih al-Bukhari 5553, Sahih Muslim 259

A well-trimmed face will bring about structure and masculinity. It may enhance your looks if you maintain it well. But also, since it is from the teachings of Rasulullah ﷺ to let it grow, you will earn good deeds for it as well, essentially causing the noor from your good to cross paths with your physical beauty.

Lastly, our Rasool ﷺ taught us a dua meant to attract Allah's noor. The dua is as follows. Ibn Abbas رضي الله عنه said that the Messenger of Allah ﷺ said:

اللَّهُمَّ اجْعَلْ فِي قَلْبِي نُورًا وَفِي لِسَانِي نُورًا وَاجْعَلْ فِي سَمْعِي نُورًا وَاجْعَلْ فِي بَصَرِي نُورًا وَاجْعَلْ مِنْ خَلْفِي نُورًا وَمِنْ أَمَامِي نُورًا وَاجْعَلْ مِنْ فَوْقِي نُورًا وَمِنْ تَحْتِي نُورًا اللَّهُمَّ أَعْطِنِي نُورًا

"O Allah, place light in my heart and light on my tongue. Place light in my hearing and light in my seeing. Place light behind me and light in front of

me. Place light above me and light below me. O
Allah, grant me light!"[157]

Appendages

Traditionally, while it may not seem 'manly' to take care of your hair, it is from the sunnah. The Prophet ﷺ taught us to ensure that the beauty of our appearance would not lack the management of our hair. He ﷺ said, *"He who has hair should honour it."*[158]

But how do you honor your hair? You must ensure its health and keep it organized. Rasulullah ﷺ would oil his hair ﷺ and sometimes even matte it with honey in order to maintain a healthy shine. And to keep his hair ﷺ neat and organized, he ﷺ would comb it in an orderly fashion. Ibn Umar رضي الله عنه said, *"The Prophet ﷺ matted his hair with honey."*[159]

---

[157] Sahih al-Bukhari 6316, Sahih Muslim 763
[158] Sunan Abi Dawud 4163 - Book 35, Hadith 5
[159] Sunan Abi Dawud 1748 - Book 11, Hadith 28

Aisha رضي الله عنها narrated, *"Allah's Messenger ﷺ used to let his head in (the house) while he was in the mosque and I would comb and oil his hair. When in I`tikaf he used not to enter the house except for a need."*[160]

Aisha رضي الله عنها also said that the Prophet ﷺ would comb his hair right to left, maintaining a consistent habit. She said, *"Allah's Messenger (Allah bless him and give him peace) used to love tayammun [beginning with his right hand, his right side and his right foot] in his ritual purification when he purified himself, in his combing when he combed his hair, and putting on his shoes when he donned them."*[161]

❖ Note: Although maintaining nice hair is from the sunnah, beware of falling into beautification ideals that are discouraged in Islam. For instance, while the

---

[160] Sahih al-Bukhari 2029 - Book 33, Hadith 5
[161] Ash-Shama'il Al-Muhammadiyah 34

Prophet of Allah ﷺ used to keep his hair ﷺ healthy and organized, he ﷺ disliked plucking gray hairs, and forbade dying hair with black dye. Jaabir ibn Abdullah رضي الله عنه reported, "*Abu Quhaafah was brought on the day of the conquest of Mecca, and his head and beard were white like 'thaghaamah' (a plant whose flowers and fruit are white). The Messenger of Allah (Peace & Blessings of Allah be upon Him) said: 'Change this with something, but avoid black.'*"[162]

Rasulullah ﷺ also told us to keep our gray hairs, as they will serve as a light for us on the Day of Judgement. He ﷺ said, "*Do not pluck grey hairs, for they will be light on the Day of Resurrection. Whoever has one hair that turns grey in Islam will have one hasanah for each grey hair and he will be raised one degree.*"[163]

---

[162] Sahih Muslim 2102b - Book 37, Hadith 124
[163] Narrated by Ibn Hibbaan, al-Albaani said in Silsilat al-Ahaadeeth as-Saheehah (3/247)

Now an equally essential part of manhood, as caring for your hair, is to maintain your nails. The Prophet ﷺ advised us to trim and groom not only our hair, but also maintain proper nail hygiene. This is something that men may ignore, causing others to view them as unhygienic. Rasulullah ﷺ said, *"Five acts are a part of natural instinct: circumcision, shaving pubic hair, plucking hair from the armpits, shortening the mustache, and clipping the nails."*[164] So as a man, take a few extra minutes to ensure that you look presentable and aren't giving off any signs of uncleanliness.

Dental Care

According to a study by the *American Academy of Cosmetic Dentistry,* over 70% of women and over 50% of men agreed that teeth are the first things

---

[164] Sahih al-Bukhari 5939, Sahih Muslim 257

they notice in a person.[165] Now it's good to get braces or Invisalign if you have crooked teeth, but more importantly, you must maintain their appearance in terms of color and health, ensuring that your smile shines bright. Failure to keep your mouth clean will lead to a tainted smile or, worse — bad breath.

To avoid these issues, Rasulullah ﷺ recommended the use of *Miswak*, also known as the *Siwak*, essentially a branch from the *Miswak tree*. He ﷺ advised us to use the Siwak as a toothbrush before every prayer. Rasulullah ﷺ said, *"If it were not that it would be difficult on my nation, then I would have ordered them to use the Siwak for each prayer."*[166] In another narration, the Prophet ﷺ said, *"I have indeed urged you with regard to the Siwak."*[167]

---

[165] Dr. Dickinson
[166] Jami at-Tirmidhi 22 - Book 1, Hadith 22
[167] Sunan an-Nasa'i 6 - Book 1, Hadith 6

But why did the Prophet ﷺ speak so highly of some stick? He ﷺ could've instead urged us towards many other things. Yet, to understand why the Siwak, it's crucial to first understand that every action holds a purpose and a benefit in Islam. And the Siwak, a stick used for oral hygiene, is no exception.

Science Behind The Miswak:

According to a study by Ranjit Patil and his team, the Siwak contains more benefits than one could count. He says, *"Many researchers have studied constituents of Miswak and found it to contain more than ten different natural chemical compounds considered essential for good oral and dental hygiene. They are fluorides, silica, tannic acid, resins, alkaloids (salvadorine), volatile oils (simgrins), sulfur, vitamin C, sodium bicarbonate, chlorides, calcium, benzylisothoicyanate, salicylic acids, sterols, trimethylamine, saponins and flavenoids."*[168]

Ranjit and his team further go on to state that these natural chemicals can lead to immense health benefits that support both your beauty and oral hygiene by keeping your teeth naturally clean through the elimination of bacteria. They say, *"Miswak have potential to inhibit plaque formation and antibacterial action against cariogenic bacteria in the oral cavity."*[169]

Smell

Not only is personal hygiene an essential aspect of self-care, but it also plays a significant role in how others perceive you. Imagine encountering someone with an unpleasant smell. You will instantly catch an impression of laziness,

---

[168] Journal of Oral Biology and Craniofacial Research
[169] Journal of Oral Biology and Craniofacial Research

negligence, or a lack of concern for cleanliness from them. This is why Rasulullah ﷺ would ensure that an unpleasant odor was never found on him ﷺ. Aisha رضي الله عنها said, *"And it would be very hard on Allah's Messenger ﷺ that a bad smell should be found on his body."*[170]

Although, if you find yourself as a man who often carries an unpleasant smell and desire to make a positive change, then fortunately for you, Rasulullah ﷺ has left behind practical guidance to assist you. In addition to taking care of your dental hygiene, which can help prevent bad breath, he ﷺ also advised us to embrace the use of fragrance, especially on special occasions or when attending gatherings. He ﷺ said, *"Verily, Allah has made this day of Friday a celebration for the Muslims. Whoever comes to*

---

[170] Sahih al-Bukhari 6972 - Book 90, Hadith 19

Friday prayer, let him bathe himself, apply perfume
if he has it, and use the toothstick."[171]

And when you apply perfume, remember that
the best scents are musk, for our Prophet ﷺ loved
them. He ﷺ said, *"The best of perfume is musk."*[172]

❖ Note: Delving deeper into cleanliness, it becomes
evident that wearing perfume alone is insufficient. It is
essential to prioritize cleanliness by regularly bathing
and wearing clean clothes. No matter how good or
strong your perfume may be, neglecting personal
hygiene or wearing old, unwashed clothes can
overpower even the most fragrant of smells.
Therefore, ensuring that both your body and clothing
are well-maintained is crucial.

The Messenger of Allah ﷺ said, *"It is a duty for*
Allah upon every Muslim to perform a ritual bath at least
once every seven days, washing his head and his

---

[171] Sunan Ibn Majah 1098
[172] Sunan an-Nasa'i 1905 - Book 21, Hadith 88

body."[173] As for the wearing of clean clothes, Imam Al-Ghazali wrote, "*This aim (of cleanliness) is an obligation upon every knowledgeable person tasked with presenting the creation with the call to Allah Almighty, that he takes care of his outward appearance so as not to compel people to avoid him.*"[174]

Speech

'*Talk too much, and they'll take you for a fool,*' a well-known piece of advice, yet one that many forget to apply when needed. It is crucial to understand that silence is power. And when you pair that silence with striking body language, strength in selected words, and dominance in your voice, you will begin to harness the power of persuasion. Rasulullah ﷺ said, "*Some eloquent speech has the influence of*

---

[173] Sahih al-Bukhari 856, Sahih Muslim 849
[174] Ihya' 'Ulum al-Din 1/137

magic. (e.g., some people refuse to do something and then a good eloquent speaker addresses them and then they agree to do that very thing after his speech)."[175]

It is very well known that the Prophet ﷺ could communicate concisely and effectively. Because he ﷺ understood that words hold power and that every utterance should be meaningful and beneficial. When people would seek his guidance ﷺ, he ﷺ would ensure they received what they sought, or at least something in return. And when he ﷺ would speak to people, his body language ﷺ would also give them respect and attention. When he ﷺ conversed with the people, he ﷺ would turn his entire body towards them to show that his full attention ﷺ was theirs. Abu Hurayra رضي الله عنه said, *"He turned completely towards people or turned his*

---

[175] Sahih al-Bukhari 5146 - Book 67, Hadith 81

back completely. I have not seen anyone like him before or since."[176]

The Prophet ﷺ would serve as a mentor, a father figure for the people. Once, when Al-Hussain رضي الله عنه asked his father, Ali ibn Abi Talib رضي الله عنه, about the various aspects of the Prophet's presence ﷺ, his father described Rasulullah ﷺ to him as such. He says, *"His munificence and his good nature ﷺ encompassed people such that he ﷺ became a father to them, and they became truly equal in his presence. His session ﷺ was a session of knowledge, forbearance, modesty, trust and patience. Voices were not raised there, there was no talk of women, and people's lapses were not broadcast. They were on a par with one another, contending with each other only in piety, humbly revering the elderly and showing compassion for the*

[176] Al-Adab Al-Mufrad 1155 - Book 47, Hadith 2

young. They were solicitous to the needy, and took good care of the stranger."[177]

Why Speak Less:

When you choose your words carefully and speak less, your voice will begin to carry more weight. People will be more likely to lend an ear when you do decide to talk, as they will recognize the value and scarcity behind your words. This intentional approach to communication allows you to foster an environment of mutual respect and understanding. When you learn to speak less and on point, you not only significantly reduce the chances of uttering words that you may regret later on, but also hide potential flaws in your character.

According to Michael Howkins, speaking excessively is a common issue amongst humans that a plethora of deep-rooted issues can cause. He says, *"80 percent of our thoughts are negative. So*

---

[177] Ash-Shama'il Al-Muhammadiyah 335 - Book 47, Hadith 7

many people speak just for the sake of speaking.
Either out of boredom, feeling uncomfortable, pride,
arrogance, fear etc. The list is endless. It's almost
like there is no filter between the mind and the
mouth with some people. Whatever idiotic thing
pops up, pops out."[178]

Fortunately for those who understand that it's
human nature to prattle endlessly, they can also
reflect upon themselves, and actively strive to burn
this unprophetic practice from their character.
Howkins mentions that you can train yourself to
speak less through meditation. He says, *"Observing*
the mind. This is a sure way to become aware of
how many thoughts are occurring in the mind at any
given time. The easiest way to accomplish this is
through meditation. Most forms of mediation will,
over time, result in a quieter mind."[179] For Muslims,

---

[178] Michael Howkins: The Art of Silence: How Speaking Less
Can Make You More Intelligent, Compassionate, and Successful
[179] Michael Howkins: The Art of Silence: How Speaking Less
Can Make You More Intelligent, Compassionate, and Successful

this meditation practice finds its expression in the form of salat. According to Fatimah Ibrahim, PhD, *"Islamic prayer, commonly represented by the Arabic term salat, is a form of meditation..."*[180]

Psychology Behind Excessive Speech:

When someone voices their thoughts excessively, it can reveal numerous flaws in their character. For example, according to Michelle C. Brooten, Bi-Polar disorder can be indicated when people talk excessively with rapid speech. He says, *"People with bipolar disorder may talk excessively with pressured or rapid speech when their brain is in a manic state."*[181] Similarly, other signs found within someone's speech can indicate different sorts of disorders including, but not limited to, anxiety

---

[180] Fatimah Ibrahim: Effect of Muslim Prayer (salat) on α Electroencephalography and Its Relationship with Autonomic Nervous System Activity
[181] Michelle C. Brooten: The Psychology Behind Excessive Talking

disorder, personality disorder, or attention deficit disorder.[182]

And, apart from revealing disturbances you might have, your excessive speech can also indicate that you are a lonely person. Because when you don't have someone to talk to at home, or many friends to spend time with, you'll often find yourself relieving bottled-up words in front of anyone you can get a hold of. Dr. Margaret Paul states, *"Sometimes people talk too much because they are lonely. When someone is willing to listen, they go on and on in an attempt to assuage their loneliness — as well as assuage the aloneness of their self-abandonment."*[183]

At the end of the day, regardless of whether or not you have these issues, it's always best to speak less and observe more. By doing so, not only will you hold your respect, but you will also be

---

[182] Michelle C. Brooten: The Psychology Behind Excessive Talking
[183] Dr. Margaret Paul: Over-Talking: The Need to Talk Too Much

adhering to the advice of Rasulullah ﷺ when he ﷺ said, *"Whoever is silent, he is saved."*[184]

Etiquette

The pinnacle of manhood lies in the embodiment of honor. Throughout this book, *Masculinity of Muhammad ﷺ: A Young Man's Handbook on Noble Masculinity,* we have delved into various facets that contribute to the development of an honorable life based on the sunnah of Rasulullah ﷺ. In this subchapter, you will learn the final laws of manhood that complete the tapestry of our selected, societal, masculine virtues. The Messenger of Allah ﷺ said, *"There is no wisdom like reflection, and no honor like good manners."*[185]

---

[184] Jami at-Tirmidhi 2501 - Book 37, Hadith 87
[185] Sunan Ibn Majah 4218 - Book 37, Hadith 119

First and foremost, it is essential to understand that the measure of your honor is tied to how honorably you treat those around you. How you interact with your family, guests, neighbors, peers, instructors, and all those who surround you plays a significant role in shaping the honor you possess. The Prophet ﷺ said, *"Whoever believes in Allah and the Last Day, let him honor his guest. Whoever believes in Allah and the Last Day, let him protect his neighbor. Whoever believes in Allah and the Last Day, let him speak goodness or remain silent."*[186] Allah says in the Quran:

وَاعْبُدُواْ اللَّهَ وَلاَ تُشْرِكُواْ بِهِ شَيْئًا وَبِالْوَالِدَيْنِ إِحْسَانًا وَبِذِي الْقُرْبَى وَالْيَتَامَى وَالْمَسَاكِينِ وَالْجَارِ ذِي الْقُرْبَى وَالْجَارِ الْجُنُبِ وَالصَّاحِبِ بِالْجَنبِ وَابْنِ السَّبِيلِ وَمَا مَلَكَتْ أَيْمَانُكُمْ إِنَّ اللَّهَ لاَ يُحِبُّ مَن كَانَ مُخْتَالاً فَخُورًا ﴿٣٦﴾

Worship Allah and associate nothing with Him, and to parents do good, and to relatives, orphans, the

---

[186] Musnad Aḥmad 6621

needy, the near neighbor, the neighbor farther away,
the companion at your side, the traveler, and those
whom your right hands possess. Indeed, Allah does
not like those who are self-deluding and boastful
(Quran 4:36)

Similar to the hadith where Rasulullah ﷺ said, *"The*
believer is a mirror to his faithful brother," your level
of manners and extent of honoring those around you
reflect your inner character.[187] They can expose
your childhood, the way you've been raised. They
can also indicate whether you're dependable,
reliable and selfless, or repellent, untrustworthy, and
selfish.

The essence of Islam and the teachings of
Rasulullah ﷺ extend far beyond recorded text and
hadith. However, those unfamiliar with his teachings
ﷺ will not read the Quran or the sunnah of

---

[187] al-Adab al-Mufrad 239

Rasulullah ﷺ in most cases. Your society, your community, however, will catch a glimpse of his blessed character and manhood ﷺ through your actions and conduct. Your character, values, and interactions become a living testament to the principles of Rasulullah's character ﷺ. So as a man, and as a Muslim, uphold strong morals. Because you are representing the best of the best ﷺ with your character.

Societal Importance of Strong Etiquette:

Although, more than just representing your leader, our Prophet, Rasulullah ﷺ, the energy you spread in the world will reflect on you. When you adhere to the prophetic teachings of manhood and strive to spread positivity, you become a beacon of light for others, inspiring those around you. People will begin to recognize your radiating energy, your compassion, and your impact on society. According to Jodi Schulz from Michigan State University,

"When you practice good manners, you're showing others that you're considerate of their feelings and respectful. You're also setting standards for other's behavior and encouraging them to treat you with the similar respect."[188]

You can also find this concept of honoring those around you in the Quran. For instance, we have the example of Ibrahim عليه السلام when angels came to him as guests in human form. He didn't know that they were angels, so he proceeded to treat them as Allah commanded him to treat guests in general; with honor and respect. Allah says in the Quran:

هَلْ أَتَاكَ حَدِيثُ ضَيْفِ إِبْرَاهِيمَ الْمُكْرَمِينَ ﴿٢٤﴾

Has the story of Abraham's honoured guests reached you [O Prophet]?
(Quran 51:24)

---

[188] Michigan State University Extension

إِذْ دَخَلُوا عَلَيْهِ فَقَالُوا سَلَامًا قَالَ سَلَامٌ قَوْمٌ مُّنكَرُونَ ﴿٢٥﴾

'Remember' when they entered his presence and greeted [him with], "Peace!" He replied, "Peace [be upon you]!" [Then he said to himself,] "[These are] an unfamiliar people."

(Quran 51:25)

فَرَاغَ إِلَى أَهْلِهِ فَجَاءَ بِعِجْلٍ سَمِينٍ ﴿٢٦﴾

Then he slipped off to his family and brought a fat [roasted] calf,

(Quran 51:26)

فَقَرَّبَهُ إِلَيْهِمْ قَالَ أَلَا تَأْكُلُونَ ﴿٢٧﴾

and placed it before them, asking, "Will you not eat?"

(Quran 51:27)

فَأَوْجَسَ مِنْهُمْ خِيفَةً قَالُوا لَا تَخَفْ وَبَشَّرُوهُ بِغُلَامٍ عَلِيمٍ ﴿٢٨﴾

[They did not eat,] so he grew fearful of them. They reassured [him], "Do not be afraid," and gave him good news of a knowledgeable son
(Quran 51:28)

Science Behind Honoring People:

When you consistently treat those around you well, actively engage with your neighbors, and act as a positive influence in your community, you will not only gain their recognition, but also experience various health benefits as well InSha'Allah.

❖ Note: Although the benefits of showing good morals will be intriguing, you must remember that your ultimate intention should be to follow Rasulullah ﷺ sincerely for the sake of Allah — not for the sake of the people.

According to Jean Kim, M.D., those people who constantly interact with others and help those around them are less likely to suffer depression. She says, *"In turn, loneliness and a lack of connection adversely affect individuals, as seen in multiple studies of health outcomes in older people, who are particularly vulnerable to isolation."*[189]

Kim continues to argue that the study examined over a thousand adults aged forty to seventy. They found that people who isolate themselves more are significantly more likely to suffer psychological issues as well. She says, *"... low levels of contact with neighbors were associated with declining levels of psychological well-being."*[190] Finally, Kim explains how our society requires fixing, as nowadays, people aren't too keen on befriending their neighbors, unlike in past societies. And this new form of isolation is creating social and societal issues on a national level.

---

[189] Jean Kim M.D: The Psychology of Neighbors
[190] Jean Kim M.D: The Psychology of Neighbors

Kim says, *"Many people, particularly introverts, note that it is increasingly difficult to make new friends after the more structured years of schooling and the tricky realm of co-workers. People have turned to social media, religious groups, volunteer organizations, groups related to hobbies, or children to connect better with new people, although the depth and meaning of those relationships can vary widely. Neighbors can offer a ready option, but people aren't always comfortable befriending them, perhaps as part of a wider issue with social connection in this country."*[191]

Expectedly enough, we find a solution to this issue of loneliness from Rasulullah's teachings ﷺ as well. He ﷺ instructed us to look after and feed our neighbor. Mujahid رضي الله عنه narrated that Abdullah bin Amr رضي الله عنه, inspired by the teachings of Rasulullah ﷺ, would make sure to share some of his

---

[191] Jean Kim M.D: The Psychology of Neighbors

food with his neighbor, regardless of the difference in religion.

Mujahid رضي الله عنه said, *"Abdullah bin Amr had a sheep slaughtered for his family, so when he came he said: 'Have you given some to our neighbor, the Jew? Have you given some to our neighbor, the Jew?' I heard the Messenger of Allah ﷺ saying: 'Jibril continued to advise me about (treating) the neighbors so (kindly and politely), that I thought he would order me (from Allah) to make them heirs.'"*[192]

Rasulullah ﷺ said also said that true believers are those who look after their neighbors' needs. He ﷺ said, *"He is not a believer whose stomach is filled while his neighbor goes hungry."*[193] Commenting on this hadith, Dawud Walid said, *"This statement should signal to the fata that he should know his neighbours and converse with them, as he cannot*

---

[192] Jami at-Tirmidhi 1943 - Book 27, Hadith 49
[193] Al-Adab Al-Mufrad 112 - Book 6, Hadith 0

*know if his neighbours are hungry without
establishing friendly relations with them first."[194]*

Humility & Modesty

Humility is the cornerstone of a man's honor, while
pride and arrogance are its destroyers. Embracing
humility allows a man to maintain dignity and
respect, fostering positive relationships and earning
the admiration of others. Because when people
notice your humility, they feel easier around you.
Consequently, they are also more likely to open up
in your presence. According to Vicki Zakrzewski,
PhD, *"When I meet someone who radiates humility,
my shoulders relax, my heart beats a little more
quietly, and something inside me lets go."[195]*

---

[194] Dawud Walid: Futuwwah and Raising Males Into Sacred
Manhood
[195] Vicki Zakrzewski: How Humility Will Make You the Greatest
Person Ever

This was precisely the character of our Prophet
ﷺ. People would be at such ease around him ﷺ,
allowing for open conversations. And going back to
the *Mentorship* subchapter in this book. In order for
society to thrive, there must be people who are
constantly helping one another rise. And to help
others solve their issues effectively, you need to first
start by building relationships with them. And one of
the most efficient ways to build relationships with
people, is to show your modesty and humility to
them.

Rasulullah ﷺ said, *"Verily, every religion has a
character and the character of Islam is modesty."*[196]
Reflected by his standard of living ﷺ, while he ﷺ
could've made dua to Allah for richness at any point
in his life ﷺ, or demanded that his followers pay him
ﷺ for his efforts ﷺ, he ﷺ instead lived a humble and
content life — a selected life of humility.

---

[196] Sunan Ibn Majah 4182

Umar ibn al-Khattab رضي الله عنه said, *"I entered the room of the Messenger of Allah, peace and blessings be upon him, while he was lying on his side over a mat. I sat down as he drew up his lower garment and he was not wearing anything else. The mat had left marks on his side. I looked at the Prophet's cupboard and I saw a handful of barely in a small amount, the same of mimosa leaves in the corner, and a leather bag hanging to the side.*

My eyes started to tear up, and the Prophet said, 'What makes you weep, son of Khattab?' I said, 'O Prophet of Allah, why should I not cry that this mat has left marks on your side and I see little in this cupboard? Caesar and Khosrau live among fruits and springs, while you are the Messenger of Allah and His chosen, yet this is your cupboard.' The Prophet said, 'O son of Khattab, are you not pleased that they are for us in the Hereafter and for them in the world?' I said, 'Of course.'"[197]

---

[197] Sahih Muslim 1479

❖ Understand: Allah isn't commanding you to seek poverty, although the poor in this world will have significantly more than the rich in the Hereafter. However, Allah commands you and I to live humbly. Share the blessings Allah has given you, be content, and most importantly, do not allow your worldly status to affect your character. If Allah is blessing you with status, do not let that negatively impact the way you treat others. Instead, remain grateful so that Allah continues to bless you with more. Allah says in the Quran:

وَإِذْ تَأَذَّنَ رَبُّكُمْ لَئِن شَكَرْتُمْ لَأَزِيدَنَّكُمْ وَلَئِن كَفَرْتُمْ إِنَّ عَذَابِي لَشَدِيدٌ ﴿٧﴾

And [remember] when your Lord proclaimed, "If you are grateful, I will certainly give you more. But if you are ungrateful, surely My punishment is severe."

(Quran 14:7)

Bear in mind that while Rasulullah ﷺ was well deserving of praise, discouraging it was something he ﷺ stayed consistent with. Instead, he ﷺ encouraged his companions to direct their praise and devotion towards Allah. Rasulullah ﷺ said, *"Do not extol me as the Christians extolled [Jesus] the son of Mary. I am merely a servant, so say: '[He is] Allah's servant and His Messenger.'"*[198]

This humility was further demonstrated again in his character ﷺ. Although the Prophet ﷺ shouldered heavy burdens and constant struggles, unlike an arrogant man, he ﷺ would still make time for his adherents ﷺ. For example, when they would invite him ﷺ, he ﷺ would accept their invitation, regardless of their status.

Anas ibn Malik رضي الله عنه said, *"The Prophet (Allah bless him and give him peace) used to be*

---

[198] Ash-Shama'il Al-Muhammadiyah 329

invited to a meal of barley bread and rancid oil, and he would accept the invitation."[199]

And even when people would seek his aid ﷺ, he ﷺ would try to prioritize their comfort first. Once, a woman came to the Prophet ﷺ seeking his advice. Rather than imposing his convenience ﷺ on her by inviting her to his meeting place ﷺ, he ﷺ allowed the woman to choose the time and place for their meeting based on her convenience. Anas ibn Malik رضي الله عنه said, *"A woman came to the Prophet (Allah bless him and give him peace) and said to him: 'I am in need of you,' so he said: 'Sit in whichever road of the city you wish, and I shall sit with you!'"*[200]

---

[199] Ash-Shama'il Al-Muhammadiyah 332
[200] Ash-Shama'il Al-Muhammadiyah 330

Desires

وَما الْحَيَاةُ الدُّنْيَا إلاَّ مَتَاعُ الْغُرُورِ ﴿١٨٥﴾

And what is the life of this world except the enjoyment of delusion.
(Quran 3:185)

As a young man in the complex landscape of modern society, you will often find yourself confronted with numerous enticing distractions that can steer you away from your faith. These obstacles, carefully disguised as appealing temptations, have the potential to overpower you and push you towards thoughts and actions that contradict the Commands of Allah. Earlier in this book, we mentioned that one of the most tiresome and destructive battles you will face are the battles against your nafs.

However, those battles grow even more grueling when natural male temptation gets involved. Submitting to your nafs can lead you down a destructive path, compromising your values, morality, and, most importantly, your imaan. Therefore, when you recognize that your nafs is mingling with your natural desires, it becomes ever-most crucial for you to seek the Help of Allah. Then, turn to the guidance of our Rasool ﷺ. For without referring back to his guidance and teachings ﷺ, these challenges will persistently grow difficult to overcome.

Although, what exactly are these desires that a man naturally carries within himself? In this chapter, *Desires,* we will delve into two pivotal temptations for men that have historically drawn us to the brink of conflict and chaos. These desires possess a captivating power that can sway hearts, influence decisions, and shape the course of civilizations: the desire for women, and the desire for power.

Women

For men, the allure of certain worldly delights is woven into the tapestry of life, evident not only within Islamic teachings but also in further cultural and non-Islamic references. Unfortunately, many of these sensual gratifications steer men towards the haram, harboring within them the seeds of self-destruction. Among these seductive lures are alcohol, drugs, gambling, smoking, and, most tempting of all, *adultery*. Rasulullah ﷺ said, *"I have not left a trial after me more harmful to men than women."*[201]

Although, this doesn't mean that women are any less important than men, or in any way are

---

[201] Sahih al-Bukhari 4808, Sahih Muslim 2740

naturally corrupt. Instead, a lot of the time, it's men who are the problem. We, as men, tend to catch feelings for females a lot faster than they do for us.

According to David Buss and April Bleske from the University of Texas at Austin, men often befriend the opposite gender hoping for a romantic or sexual relationship, not just to be friends with them. They say, *"For men, more than for women, one function of opposite-sex friendship is to provide sexual access to the opposite sex."*[202]

❖ Understand: You find that most destructive temptations often possess a gender-neutral appeal, ensnaring both men and women. They may include an inclination towards alcohol, drugs, riba, etc. However, adultery, *zina* is an allure that transcends temporal boundaries. Zina can be considered one of the greatest temptations that have corrupted society

---

[202] David M. Buss and April L. Bleske: Can men and women be just friends

throughout history, most notably captivating the hearts of men. And Allah has set clear boundaries against the forbidden fruit of zina to the extent that He has also forbidden actions that could lead to it. Allah says in the Quran:

وَلاَ تَقْرَبُواْ الزِّنَى إِنَّهُ كَانَ فَاحِشَةً وَسَاء سَبِيلاً ﴿٣٢﴾

And do not approach unlawful sexual intercourse. Indeed, it is ever an immorality and is evil as a way.

(Quran 17:32)

Now, what could happen if you actually commit zina? Will you just be committing a sin like any other? No, rather, zina is no laughing matter, contradictory to what society may teach. If you fall into zina, your noor will darken, and your imaan will be drained from your body. I.e., when imaan leaves your body, you will find yourself slipping out of the fold of Islam. Rasulullah ﷺ said, *"The adulterer is not a believer while he is committing adultery."*[203]

❖ Understand: Envision yourself entangled in the act of zina. Imagine that as this sin's weight burdens your conscience, Allah sends the Angel of Death to claim your soul. What will unfold then? Should death claim you while engaged in this forbidden act, according to the words of Rasulullah ﷺ, the mantle of true belief slips away from your being. Picture yourself living with imaan, following the Commands of Allah your entire life, just to throw it out the window for a few moments of pleasure. Ask yourself, what then? If you do not die as a Muslim, then what will become of your Hereafter?

And yes, you may be thinking to yourself, *'Well, that's easier said than done. I struggle with women. How can I practically adhere to this advice?'* To answer your question, let's look back to the life of Rasulullah

---

[203] Sahih al-Bukhari 2475, Sahih Muslim 57

🕋. What advice did our Prophet 🕋 give to withstand the allures of zina?

The Man Who Sought Permission

During the life of Rasulullah 🕋, a young man once approached him 🕋, seeking his permission to commit zina. The companions present there were left speechless. How could a man blatantly walk up to the Prophet 🕋 and seek his permission 🕋 to commit such a sin?

However, the Prophet 🕋 didn't get angry, nor did he 🕋 punish the man. He 🕋 didn't call him crazy or yell at him. Instead, the Prophet 🕋 simply said *no*. Then, he 🕋 went on to explain his *no* to the man in a manner, that, after this meeting, the man went back, never wishing for zina again.

The story is reported by Abu Umamah رضي الله عنه. He says, "*A young man came to the Prophet, peace and blessings be upon him, and he said, 'O*

Messenger of Allah, give me permission to commit adultery.' The people turned to rebuke him, saying, 'Quiet! Quiet!' The Prophet said, 'Come here.' The young man came close and he told him to sit down.

The Prophet said, 'Would you like that for your mother?' The man said, 'No, by Allah, may I be sacrificed for you.' The Prophet said, 'Neither would people like it for their mothers. Would you like that for your daughter?' The man said, 'No, by Allah, may I be sacrificed for you.' The Prophet said, 'Neither would people like it for their daughters. Would you like that for your sister?' The man said, 'No, by Allah, may I be sacrificed for you.' The Prophet said, 'Neither would people like it for their sisters. Would you like that for your aunts?' The man said, 'No, by Allah, may I be sacrificed for you.' The Prophet said, 'Neither would people like it for their aunts.' Then, the Prophet placed his hand on him and he said:

اللَّهُمَّ اغْفِرْ ذَنْبَهُ وَطَهِّرْ قَلْبَهُ وَحَصِّنْ فَرْجَهُ

223

'O Allah, forgive his sins, purify his heart, and guard his chastity.'

After that, the young man never again inclined to anything sinful."[204]

❖ Understand: While it should be noted that the issue of zina is severe and requires the utmost attention, especially in today's time, it's also crucial to understand that its allure has existed throughout history. Men before you have struggled, and men after you will continue to struggle with its seductive call, leading the weak-minded amongst you to Hell. But, your struggle will be worth it in the end. The Prophet ﷺ said, *"The Paradise is surrounded by hardships and the Hell-Fire is surrounded by temptations."*[205]

---

[204] Musnad Ahmad 21708
[205] Sahih Muslim 2822 - Book 53, Hadith 1

If you find yourself amongst those entangled in the web of temptation, grappling with zina in any measure, take heed to the wisdom of Rasulullah ﷺ as you will find in the following list. You will undoubtedly find in his teachings ﷺ an illuminated path toward resolution and success.

1. First and foremost, engrave in your heart that Allah is All-Seeing. He is the One who will grant your wishes, forgive your sins, and will love you. He has created you, bestowed you with more blessings than many, fed you, clothed you, and loves you more than your mother. How does it make you feel knowing that you are disobeying His commands in His presence when you sin?

   So embrace the consciousness of His watchful gaze, for it serves as a guiding light and a protective shield against the allure of sin. In every moment, remember that your deeds are laid bare before Allah, who is your Lord and mine.

2. As a secondary measure, exercise caution by deliberately distancing yourself from environments, venues, rooms, or people that could ignite the flame of zina within you. Seek refuge in Allah, and seek the company of those who will constantly remind you of Allah's presence.

   Surround yourself with people who uplift and inspire you to traverse the righteous path — brothers who fear Allah, who will ensure to keep you in check if you ever begin to slip. As the saying goes, '*Spend your days with five losers, and you'll soon become the sixth. Spend your days with five winners, and you'll eventually become the sixth.*'

3. After applying the first two measures of controlling your temptations, you'll be able to

adhere to the next piece of advice from Rasulullah ﷺ. He ﷺ instructed us, men, to either get married if we have the means, or fast in order to control our desires. He ﷺ said, *"O young men, whoever among you can afford it, let him get married, and whoever cannot, let him fast, for it will be a shield for him."*[206]

As marriage may seem out of the question for many young men fighting the call to zina, the more suitable approach would be fasting. However, remember that the Prophet ﷺ is not telling you to fast every day outside of Ramadan. On the contrary, he ﷺ shows you the ideal days to fast, which are Mondays and Thursdays.

Aisha رضي الله عنها said, *"The Prophet used to try to fast on Mondays and Thursdays."*[207] And when he ﷺ was asked why he ﷺ fasted on Mondays, he ﷺ said, *"That is the day on which I*

---

[206] Sahih al-Bukhari 5065 - Book 67, Hadith 3
[207] Jami` at-Tirmidhi 745 - Book 8, Hadith 64

was born and the day on which I received Revelation."[208] As for Thursdays, he ﷺ said, along with Mondays, Thursdays are the days when deeds are presented to Allah. He ﷺ said, *"Deeds are presented on Monday and Thursday, and I love that my deeds be presented while I am fasting."*[209]

4. Lastly, the fourth piece of practical advice from Rasulullah ﷺ is to lower your gaze regardless of your marital status. Because if you cannot see haram, you are less likely to think about haram as well. And when the thoughts of zina aren't constantly bombarding your nafs, you are less likely to approach it. Allah says in the Quran:

قُل لِّلْمُؤْمِنِينَ يَغُضُّوا مِنْ أَبْصَارِهِمْ وَيَحْفَظُوا فُرُوجَهُمْ ذَلِكَ أَزْكَى لَهُمْ إِنَّ اللَّهَ خَبِيرٌ بِمَا يَصْنَعُونَ ﴿٣٠﴾

---

[208] Riyad as-Salihin 1255
[209] Jami` at-Tirmidhi 747 - Book 8, Hadith 66

Tell the believing men to lower their gaze and guard their chastity. That is purer for them. Surely Allah is All-Aware of what they do.
(Quran 24:30)

❖ Understand: Although these temptations exist, Rasulullah ﷺ taught us ways to avoid them. However, if you still fall into sin, remember that all hope is not lost. Allah's mercy is still there. Allah's forgiveness can still be attained. Although you must seek it. Follow your sins with righteous acts and seek sincere forgiveness, knowing that Allah will forgive you regardless of your sin, InSha'Allah.

Rasulullah ﷺ said, *"Have taqwa (fear) of Allah wherever you may be, and follow up a bad deed with a good deed which will wipe it out, and behave well towards the people."*[210] He ﷺ also said, *"One is not a*

---

[210] Hadith 18, 40 Hadith an-Nawawi

stubborn sinner if he sincerely seeks forgiveness from Allah, even if he were to do it seventy times in a day."[211]

So seek the solace of forgiveness from Allah, ever mindful that Allah's mercy stands as a beacon of hope for all. Let it resonate within your mind that no sin, regardless of its weight or magnitude, possesses the power to overshadow Allah's mercy. Allah affirms this in the Quran when He says:

وَمَن يَعْمَلْ سُوءًا أَوْ يَظْلِمْ نَفْسَهُ ثُمَّ يَسْتَغْفِرِ اللَّهَ يَجِدِ اللَّهَ غَفُورًا رَّحِيمًا ﴿١١٠﴾

And whoever does a wrong or wrongs himself but then seeks forgiveness of Allah will find Allah Forgiving and Merciful.

(Quran 4:110)

Leadership

Have you ever heard the saying, *'Leadership is bestowed, not taken?'* Why do you think they say that? It's because as a man, you will face the desire for leadership and power. Naturally, as a man, you will want to be better and more powerful than others. However, this is not what Rasulullah ﷺ advised. In a world where audacious and underserving people may assert their jurisdiction, you must acknowledge that their grasp on power often proves fleeting and insubstantial. Rarely does their reign yield fruitful outcomes.

True leadership, rooted in worthiness and purpose, lies in the ability to emulate the noble example of our Rasool ﷺ. His model ﷺ transcends mere dominance and assumes a mantle of inspiration, serving as a beacon of hope for all who follow him ﷺ. This is what you and I must strive to embody. A worthy leader becomes the pillar upon which others lean, entrusted with their hopes and aspirations.

So as a man, strive to inspire and serve those around you. And if the people see fit, they will set you in a position of leadership. Else you continue with your selfless endeavors. Rasulullah ﷺ said, *"Verily, the leader is only a shield behind whom they fight and he protects them. If he commands the fear of Allah the Exalted and justice, then he will have a reward. If he commands something else, then it will be against him."*[212]

❖ Understand: Allah will reward the righteous leaders, for they serve the weak and protect their adherents. However, leaders who strive as hypocrites and misguiders, breaking trust and acting on their desires, will face severe humiliation and disgrace. Rasulullah ﷺ said, *"Woe to the rulers! Woe to the authorities! Woe to the trustees! Some people will wish their forelocks were*

_____

[212] Sahih Muslim 1841

hanging from the star of Pleiades on the Day of Resurrection rather than had been responsible for anything."[213]

For men, the allure of leadership can often exert a powerful temptation. When leadership is at the tip of your fingers, Shaytaan seeks to ensnare you with false ambition, pride, and ego. Yet, as a man, you must remain steadfast and remember your place in society. You are called to introspect, reflect upon your skills and abilities, and utilize them to better the community as a whole. Although, if your skills fit the position of leadership, and there seems to be no one more worthy than you, then by all means, strive towards it. However, it is essential that you first work to find the most deserving candidate for that position.

---

[213] Musnad Ahmad 8612

The Successor

In the aftermath of the passing of Rasulullah ﷺ, the ummah found itself in a state of confusion, pondering who would assume the mantle of leadership. The Ansar from Medina argued that the caliph should be from amongst them. They believed that their people were most deserving of the title. So when the Ansar learned about the death of Rasulullah ﷺ, they began discussing amongst themselves the matter of appointing a caliph.[214]

On the other hand, there were the Quraish, who the Prophet ﷺ was originally from. They wanted the caliph to be from amongst them. So while the conflicting arguments proved a temporary setback, the sahaba resolved the issue rather quickly, agreeing that the caliph should be from the Quraish. Because although the Ansar wanted the caliph to be from them, they weren't arrogant people.

---

[214] Abu Bakr As-Siddeeq: His Life & Times P.200

On the contrary, the Ansar were amongst the best of people. Rasulullah ﷺ said, *"None loves the Ansar but a believer, and none hates them but a hypocrite. Whoever loves them, Allah will love him. Whoever hates them, Allah will hate him."*[215]

Then, upon resolving their first disagreement, another issue quickly arose among the Muslims. However, the second dispute did not occur due to a lack of worthy candidates or conflicting sides. But instead, the companions didn't know who to appoint because the most deserving of them shunned the title. They simply did not want to deal with that responsibility. They understood that a leader's sole purpose is to put the needs of his adherents over his own. And that he would be held accountable for anything less. Rasulullah ﷺ said, *"The leader of a people is their servant."*[216] Yet, after initially declining the position, Abu Bakr رضي الله عنه was

---

[215] Sahih al-Bukhari 3783, Sahih Muslim 75
[216] Hadith 34, 40 Hadith Shah Waliullah

compelled to take the burden by the rest of the sahaba.

❖ Note: Some argue that it is best to leave leadership if you can. Instead, utilize your energy and time to help, serve, and benefit those around you — just as the Prophet ﷺ taught by example. Nonetheless, despite the weighty burden accompanying the position of leadership, it does not negate the pursuit of impactful work for Muslims. On the contrary, while leadership comes with its struggles, Rasulullah ﷺ speaks about a man who Allah will guide for humanity. He ﷺ tells us about a true leader's impact when he ﷺ talks about the *Guided One*.

Rasulullah ﷺ said in a very famous hadith, *"Verily, Allah will raise up in this nation at the beginning of every century someone who will renew their religion.*[217] I.e., a man who will reawaken and rejuvenate the sleeping Muslims of the time. However, as Muslim men, it is not your role to question or passively wait for the arrival of the Guided One. Instead, your duty lies in actively striving to impact and serve those around you. Take part in philanthropy, volunteering, dawah work, etc.

And while you may work, your aspirations may not always impact the entire Ummah, which is okay. But by doing your part, you will still have an effect. You will still create change, and that is what the ummah desperately needs! It needs every able Muslim striving to impact and benefit those around him. Serve the needs of your neighbors in your neighborhood, the needs of the homeless in your city, the needs of the lost Muslims in your community, and so on. Spread goodness, serve the people, and stand as beacons of light for all those around you.

---

[217] Sunan Abi Dawud 4291

Success

A man's journey toward manhood is heavily intertwined with his ability to succeed in life. This success can be defined in a plethora of ways, not limited to wealth or fame. It can be defined by your ambitions and goals. And regardless of what those goals may be, fortunately for you, Rasulullah ﷺ outlined numerous habits and principles that led him ﷺ to success both in the Sight of Allah, and within society. This chapter, *Success,* however, will delve into two specific deeds that are the most beloved to Allah, as well as the single change you must bring into your life in order to crush your goals.

And it's crucial to understand that your success can come only through Allah. Do you honestly believe that your work alone will make good things happen without Allah willing it? When Prophet

Shu'aib السلام عليه was dealing with his people's insults and sarcastic questioning, he stood firm because he understood that unless Allah willed otherwise, ultimate success would be with him. His story is mentioned in the Quran when Allah says:

قَالُواْ يَا شُعَيْبُ أَصَلَاتُكَ تَأْمُرُكَ أَن نَّتْرُكَ مَا يَعْبُدُ آبَاؤُنَا أَوْ أَن نَّفْعَلَ فِي أَمْوَالِنَا مَا نَشَاء إِنَّكَ لَأَنتَ الْحَلِيمُ الرَّشِيدُ ﴿٨٧﴾

They asked [sarcastically], "O Shu'aib! Does your prayer command you that we should abandon what our forefathers worshipped or give up managing our wealth as we please? Indeed, you are such a tolerant, sensible man!"
(Quran 11:87)

قَالَ يَا قَوْمِ أَرَأَيْتُمْ إِن كُنتُ عَلَىَ بَيِّنَةٍ مِّن رَّبِّي وَرَزَقَنِي مِنْهُ رِزْقًا حَسَنًا وَمَا أُرِيدُ أَنْ أُخَالِفَكُمْ إِلَى مَا أَنْهَاكُمْ عَنْهُ إِنْ أُرِيدُ إِلاَّ الإِصْلاَحَ مَا اسْتَطَعْتُ وَمَا تَوْفِيقِي إِلاَّ بِاللهِ عَلَيْهِ تَوَكَّلْتُ وَإِلَيْهِ أُنِيبُ ﴿٨٨﴾

He said, "O my people! Consider if I stand on a clear proof from my Lord and He has blessed me with a good provision from Him. I do not want to do what I am forbidding you from. I only intend reform to the best of my ability. **My success comes only through Allah.** In Him I trust and to Him I turn.
(Quran 11:88)

Salat

يَا أَيُّهَا الَّذِينَ آمَنُواْ اسْتَعِينُواْ بِالصَّبْرِ وَالصَّلاَةِ إِنَّ اللَّهَ مَعَ الصَّابِرِينَ ﴿١٥٣﴾

O believers! Seek comfort in patience and prayer. Allah is truly with those who are patient.
(Quran 2:153)

The observance of salat at its proper time is considered one of Allah's two most beloved deeds. Abdullah رضي الله عنه once asked the Prophet ﷺ which deeds are most beloved to Allah, to which he

ﷺ replied, "*To offer the prayers at their early stated fixed times.*"[218] Based on this hadith, you see that, on one hand, you will find the rewards and benefits of prayer, such as it being one of the most beloved deeds to Allah. But on the other hand, you also find the consequences of ignoring your mandatory salats. Rasulullah ﷺ said, *"That which differentiates us from the disbelievers and hypocrites is our performance of salat. He who abandons it, becomes a disbeliever."*[219]

Therefore, while some sins deter your heart from worshiping Allah, others, such as ignoring your salats, can take you out of Islam entirely. Understand that after the *Shahada*, salat stands as a fundamental and indispensable pillar of Islam. Therefore, when you look at the life of Rasulullah ﷺ, you'll find that, unlike many of us, he ﷺ and his

---

[218] Sahih al-Bukhari 527 - Book 9, Hadith 6
[219] Riyad as-Salihin 1079

companions eagerly looked forward to salat, as it was the coolness of their eyes.

Rasulullah ﷺ said, *"There are five prayers that Allah has prescribed for His slaves. Whoever comes with them, not having missed any of them out of recognition of their importance, has a promise from Allah that He will admit him to Paradise."*[220]

Now what about those benefits that are separate from salat but surround it in the same time frame? First, we know that the adhan and iqamah are given shortly before the prayer starts. Rasulullah ﷺ gave glad tidings saying that dua is not rejected during this time. He ﷺ said, *"Du'a is not rejected between the adhan and iqamah, so engage in du'a (supplication)."*[221]

Next, when you pray salat, you essentially engage in an intimate conversation with Allah. The

---

[220] Abu Dawood 1420 and an-Nasaa'i 461
[221] Narrated by al-Tirmidhi, 212; Abu Dawud, 437; Ahmad, 12174

Prophet ﷺ said, *"When one of you stands in prayer, he is conversing with his Lord, so let one of you know what he is saying to his Lord and do not raise your voices above one another in reciting when praying."*[222]

Following the actual salat, Rasulullah ﷺ recommended staying seated, and engaging in the Remembrance of Allah, for the angels in the sky pray for your forgiveness until you leave your spot. He ﷺ said, *"The angels keep on asking Allah's forgiveness for anyone of you, as long as he is at his Musalla (praying place) and he does not pass wind (Hadath). They say, 'O Allah! Forgive him, O Allah! be Merciful to him.'"*[223]

❖ Understand: When there is virtue in the actions before salat, in the actions during salat, and in the actions after salat, what exemplary virtues must be present in

---

[222] Narrated by Ahmad 4928 and classed as saheeh by Shu'ayb al-Arna'oot in Tahqeeq al-Musnad
[223] al-Bukhaari 445 and Muslim 649

salat itself? And since the spiritual benefits are so heavy, it only begs the question: what must be the physical value of salat that impacts our worldly life?

Science Behind Salat:

Salat will help you maintain ideal body health, as well as significantly improve your mental abilities. According to Sami Saleh Al Abdulwahab, PT, PhD, and his team, *"Islamic 'salat' prayers include both spiritual meditation and physical movements of various parts of the body and they are believed to improve equilibrium, balance, and joint flexibility as well as maintain lower limb performance…"*[224]

To understand how salat, which takes up a few mins of your day, constitutes for these health benefits, you must understand how the study was conducted. Abdulwahab's analysis was based on testing the physical motions in salat, as well as the

---

[224] Alabdulwahab: Physical Activity Associated with Prayer Regimes Improves Standing Dynamic Balance of Healthy People

mental state of participants before and after praying. They tested the participants through various aspects of movement that related to joint, muscle, and brain functions.

They say, *"Religious meditation and prayers have been found to promote relaxation and a healthier, more balanced condition of the human mind and body. Studies on the benefits of 'salat' have revealed that it improves not only spiritual well-being, but also mental and physical health, improving muscle strength, joint mobility and blood circulation, when performed correctly and with the right postures."*[225]

Tahajjud

The concept of Tahajjud has been touched upon earlier in this book. We mentioned that Salat al-

---

[225] Alabdulwahab: Physical Activity Associated with Prayer Regimes Improves Standing Dynamic Balance of Healthy People

Tahajjud (the Tahajjud prayer) is one of the best deeds you can perform. And the Tahajjud time is one of the best times to engage in dua. Imam Ash-Shafi'i said, *"The dua made at Tahajjud is like an arrow which does not miss its target."*[226]

But what exactly is Tahajjud? Tahajjud time refers to the last third of the night, considered the most significant portion of the night for Muslims. During the last third of the night, Allah descends to the lowest Heaven, calling His servants to seek whatever they desire from Him. Rasulullah ﷺ said, *"Allah descends every night to the lowest heaven when one-third of the first part of the night is over and says: I am the Lord; I am the Lord: who is there to supplicate Me so that I answer him? Who is there to beg of Me so that I grant him? Who is there to beg forgiveness from Me so that I forgive him? He continues like this till the day breaks."*[227]

---

[226] Imam Ash-Shafi'i
[227] Sahih Muslim 758b - Book 6, Hadith 202

Yet, many of us ignore this Call, continuing with our sleep. Although, there are practical steps that can be taken in order to apply this prophetic practice to your life. Since you're just starting, one way to catch Tahajjud is to wake up about 20 minutes before Fajr salat starts. Wake up, make wudu, pray two rak'ah nafil, and make dua to Allah. Then as Fajr time starts, finish up your duas, pray Fajr, and either get your day started or go back to sleep. Since Tahajjud time ends as Fajr time begins, you can pray both salats back-to-back. Although it is better to have a brief pause or some differentiation, such as engaging in dua, reciting the Quran, or simply taking a short break between Tahajjud and Fajr to mark the end of one prayer and the beginning of another.

❖ Note: Praying Tahajjud and Fajr back-to-back is one of the easiest and most basic ways to pray Tahajjud, although still effective. If you wish, however, to increase the power of your dua at Tahajjud time, then increase the worship surrounding your Tahajjud salat. Before starting your Tahajjud prayer, consider engaging in extra dhikr, reading more Quran, seeking Allah's forgiveness for mental clarity, etc. Then, as you begin your actual prayer, consider lengthening it by reciting more verses. The longer you sincerely stand in Tahajjud, the more significant impact your duas can have.

Rasulullah ﷺ said, *"Whoever stands to pray with ten verses will never be recorded among the negligent. Whoever stands with a hundred verses will recorded among those devoutly obedient to Allah. Whoever stands with a thousand verses will be recorded among those with tremendous rewards."*[228]

Now, envision the possibilities unfolding when you consistently dedicate your time to reciting a

---

[228] Sunan Abi Dawud 1398

thousand, a hundred, or even just ten verses a night, during Tahajjud. This noble pursuit has the potential to unlock a multitude of virtues, allowing you to soar to new heights in your spiritual journey. Consequently, by praying Tahajjud consistently in the ideal fashion, your virtue will begin exemplifying by overlapping with other deeds of great magnitude as well. These deeds can include:

- Praying Salat
- Being Consistent
- Reciting 1000 verses
- Making Dua (Dua is worship)
- Reading Quran

❖ Understand: Although the Prophet ﷺ said the one who recites 1000 verses would have tremendous rewards, he ﷺ did not limit himself to only that. His Tahajjud ﷺ, and his voluntary salats ﷺ could take hours. Once Abdullah رضي الله عنه, a companion of the Prophet ﷺ,

saw the Prophet ﷺ praying Tahajjud. Wanting to pray behind his role model ﷺ, he joined the Prophet ﷺ in his prayer. Little did he know how long the Prophet's Tahajjud prayers ﷺ actually were. He described the Tahajjud, saying that it was so lengthy, that his feet could hardly bear standing through it.

Abu-Wail رضي الله عنه narrated that Abdullah رضي الله عنه said, *"One night I offered the Tahajjud prayer with the Prophet ﷺ and he kept on standing till an ill-thought came to me. We said, 'What was the ill-thought?' He said, 'It was to sit down and leave the Prophet (standing).'"*[229]

Parents

Before you skip this subchapter, thinking you'll find another guilt-trip session in these pages, you must

---

[229] Sahih al-Bukhari 1135 - Book 19, Hadith 16

realize that you are not alone in pain — especially if
you are a first-generation child growing up abroad.
We've mentioned the hadith where Rasulullah ﷺ
says praying salat at its prescribed time is the best
deed in the Eyes of Allah. However, the hadith
continues. Abdullah رضي الله عنه said, "*I asked the
Prophet ﷺ 'Which deed is the dearest to Allah?' He
replied, 'To offer the prayers at their early stated
fixed times.' I asked, 'What is the next (in
goodness)?' He replied, '**To be good and dutiful to
your parents**'*"[230]

Sometimes you may feel like an outsider, adopted
by your parents, and even though they look like you,
they don't understand you. It seems this way
because they are 'backward and nonsensical
people,' and their core mission is to 'anger you to
the grave'. You rebel, you fight, and you may even
go behind their backs, for you are young and

[230] Sahih al-Bukhari 527 - Book 9, Hadith 6

unconquerable. This is wrong. Regardless of what 'pain' you see them causing you, understand that it is for your benefit. And it is your duty to ensure promising treatment of them. Allah says in the Quran:

وَقَضَى رَبُّكَ أَلاَّ تَعْبُدُواْ إِلاَّ إِيَّاهُ وَبِالْوَالِدَيْنِ إِحْسَانًا إِمَّا يَبْلُغَنَّ عِندَكَ الْكِبَرَ أَحَدُهُمَا أَوْ كِلاَهُمَا فَلاَ تَقُل لَّهُمَآ أُفٍّ وَلاَ تَنْهَرْهُمَا وَقُل لَّهُمَا قَوْلاً كَرِيمًا ﴿٢٣﴾

And your Lord has decreed that you worship not except Him, and to parents, good treatment. Whether one or both of them reach old age [while] with you, say not to them [so much as], "uff," and do not repel them but speak to them a noble word.
(Quran 17:23)

وَاخْفِضْ لَهُمَا جَنَاحَ الذُّلِّ مِنَ الرَّحْمَةِ وَقُل رَّبِّ ارْحَمْهُمَا كَمَا رَبَّيَانِي صَغِيرًا ﴿٢٤﴾

And be humble with them out of mercy, and pray,
"My Lord! Be merciful to them as they raised me
when I was young."
(Quran 17:24)

However, why is this subchapter under *Success?*
How do parents play a role in your success, apart
from raising and pushing you toward it? Well, they
actually occupy one of the most significant roles in
your success, both for this world and the next.

Your treatment of them can either attract the
Mercy of Allah and ease, or continued difficulties
and struggles. Then in the Hereafter, your actions
towards them can either get you into the gardens of
Heaven, or land you in the pits of Hell. Abu
Umamah رضي الله عنه narrated that a man asked
Rasulullah ﷺ, *"O Allah's Messenger ﷺ, what are the
rights of parents over their child?"* He ﷺ replied
saying, *"They are your Paradise and your Hell."*[231]

---

[231] Sunan Ibn Majah 3662 - Book 33, Hadith 6

Conversely, how can the treatment of your parents affect your worldly life? What can Allah do for you when you sacrifice your comfort and your needs for the sake of those who raised you?

The answer is found in the story of Uwais Al-Qarani. He was a man from Yemen, from the tribe of Qaran, who devoted much of his life in service to his mother. Uwais never met the Prophet ﷺ due to his responsibility of caring for his sick mother, although his heart deeply desired to meet the Rasool ﷺ. After years of yearning to see his Beloved ﷺ, an opportunity arose where people from Yemen were going to Medina to meet the Prophet ﷺ.

However, as eagerly as he wanted to visit and see the Prophet ﷺ, Uwais stayed back in Yemen due to his sick mother. She didn't have anyone else to take care of her. The Prophet ﷺ knew about Uwais and his condition, and he ﷺ knew that Uwais chose to stay with his mother over meeting him ﷺ. So he ﷺ said to his companions, who were already the best of Muslims, to ask Uwais to seek Allah's forgiveness on their behalf if they ever meet him. He ﷺ told them that his relationship with Allah resided at exponentially high levels due to his devotion towards his mother.

Umar Ibn Al-Khattab رضي الله عنه said, "I heard Allah's Messenger ﷺ as saying: Worthy amongst the successors would be a person who would be called Uwais. He would have his mother (living with him) and he would have (a small) sign of leprosy. Ask him to beg pardon for you (from Allah)."[232] Then eventually, the Prophet ﷺ passed away without ever meeting Uwais. However, years later Uwais would eventually visit the sahaba. And the story is as follows.

Usair bin Jabir رضي الله عنه said, "When the people of Yemen came, Umar started asking people in the group, 'Is there anyone among you from Qaran,' until he came to [the tribe of Qaran] and

---

232 Sahih Muslim 2542b - Book 44, Hadith 320

said: 'Who are you?' They said: 'Qaran.' Umar's reins — or Uwais`s reins — fell and one of them picked them up and gave them to the other. Umar recognized him and said: 'What is your name?' He said: 'I am Uwais,' [Umar] said: 'Do you have a mother?' [Uwais] said: 'Yes.' [Umar] said: 'Did you have any whiteness [leprosy]?' He said: 'Yes, but I prayed to Allah, may He be glorified and exalted, and He took it away, except for an area the size of a dirham near my navel, so that I would remember my Lord.'

Umar said to him: 'Pray for forgiveness for me.' He said: 'Rather you should pray for forgiveness for me; you are the Companion of the Messenger of Allah ﷺ.' Umar رضي الله عنه said: 'I heard the Messenger of Allah ﷺ say: The best of the Tabi`een will be a man called Uwais who has a mother, and he has some whiteness, then he prayed to Allah, may He be glorified and exalted, and He took it away, except for an area the size of a dirham near his navel.' So he prayed for forgiveness for him, *then he disappeared in a group of people and no one knew where he ended up."[233]*

❖ Understand: The sahaba were the best of Muslims. They were exalted to such an extent that Allah guaranteed them Paradise while on Earth — an honor only a handful of people bear. Allah says in the Quran about the sahaba:

جَزَاؤُهُمْ عِندَ رَبِّهِمْ جَنَّاتُ عَدْنٍ تَجْرِي مِن تَحْتِهَا الْأَنْهَارُ خَالِدِينَ فِيهَا أَبَدًا رَّضِيَ اللَّهُ عَنْهُمْ وَرَضُوا عَنْهُ ذَٰلِكَ لِمَنْ خَشِيَ رَبَّهُ ﴿٨﴾

Their reward with their Lord will be Gardens of Eternity, under which rivers flow, to stay there for ever and ever. Allah is pleased with them and they are pleased with Him. This is [only] for those in awe of their Lord.

(Quran 98:8)

---

[233] Musnad Ahmad 266, 267

And Umar Ibn Al-Khattab رضي الله عنه was amongst the best of the sahaba. Rasulullah ﷺ said that if he ﷺ were not the last Prophet of Allah, and that if there were to be another prophet after him ﷺ, it would have been Umar Ibn Al-Khattab رضي الله عنه. He ﷺ said, *"If there was to have a Prophet after me, it would have been Umar bin Al-Khattab."*[234]

So to say that the Messenger of Allah ﷺ told Umar رضي الله عنه a man of such virtue, to request Uwais Al-Qarani, a man who'd never even met the Prophet ﷺ, to seek forgiveness from Allah on his behalf, stands at such a great extent. Not only do we see that Allah favored Uwais, but his dua was indeed powerful, as shown when he made dua to Allah to cure his leprosy, an incurable disease at the time.

Allah knows best, but we see that Uwais was able to reach such a high position in the Eyes of

---

[234] Jami at-Tirmidhi 3686 - Book 49, Hadith 82

Allah simply due to his unconditional loyalty and devotion to his mother. And this would make sense. Because the Prophet ﷺ said, *"The pleasure of the Lord is in the pleasure of the parents, and the displeasure of the Lord is in the displeasure of the parents."*[235]

---

[235] Sunan al-Tirmidhi 1899

Masculinity of Muhammad ﷺ

A Young Man's Handbook on Noble Masculinity

Selected Bibliography

Aggarwal, Ricky. "The sunnah of smelling good – It's for men as much
as women." *Aquila Style*, 13 June 2019, https://aquila-
style.com/the-sunnah-of-smelling-good-its-for-men-as-much-
as-women/#note2.

Ahmad, Musnad Imam. "Hadith on Courage: Let not fear stop you from
speaking truth." *Faith in Allah*, 20 December 2013,
https://www.abuaminaelias.com/dailyhadithonline/2013/12/20/c
ourage-let-not-fear-stop-you/.

Ahmad, Musnad Imam. "Hadith on Faith: Honor the guest, guard the
neighbor." *Faith in Allah*, 13 September 2022,
https://www.abuaminaelias.com/dailyhadithonline/2022/09/13/h
onor-the-guest/.

Alabdulwahab, Sami Saleh, et al. "Physical activity associated with
prayer regimes improves standing dynamic balance of healthy
people." 2013, pp. 1565-1568. *National Library of Medicine*,
doi: 10.1589/jpts.25.1565.

al-Ansari, Muḥammad ibn Abd Allah. "Umar on Gluttony: A large belly is
a punishment, not a blessing." *Faith in Allah*, 4 March 2018,
https://www.abuaminaelias.com/dailyhadithonline/2018/03/04/b
ig-belly-punishment-not-blessing/.

al-Bayhaqi, Abu Bakr Ahmad ibn al-Husayn. "Ali on Iman: Faith is a light
in the heart, hypocrisy is darkness." *Faith in Allah*, 15 February
2021,
https://www.abuaminaelias.com/dailyhadithonline/2021/02/15/a
li-iman-light/.

al-Bayhaqi, Al-Hakim Abu Bakr Ahmad ibn 'Ali ibn Thabit. "Abdullah on
Medicine: Use the Quran and honey for healing." *Faith in Allah*,
20 April 2021,
https://www.abuaminaelias.com/dailyhadithonline/2021/04/20/q
uran-honey/.

al-Bazzar, Abu Bakr Ahmad ibn al-Husayn. "Hadith on Grudges: Let go
of hatred, malice, and enmity." *Faith in Allah*, 24 June 2016,
https://www.abuaminaelias.com/dailyhadithonline/2016/06/24/d
rop-your-grudges/.

al-Bukhari, Muhammad ibn Ismail. "Al-Adab Al-Mufrad 112 - Neighbours
- كتاب الْجَار. -" *Sunnah.com*, https://sunnah.com/adab:112.

al-Bukhari, Muhammad ibn Ismail. "Al-Adab Al-Mufrad 1155 - Behaviour
with people - كتاب تعامل الناس. -" *Sunnah.com*,
https://sunnah.com/adab:1155.

al-Bukhari, Muhammad ibn Ismail. "Al-Adab Al-Mufrad 252 -

Cheerfulness Towards People - كتاب الانبساط إلى النَّاس."

Sunnah.com, https://sunnah.com/adab:252.

al-Bukhari, Muhammad ibn Ismail. "Al-Adab Al-Mufrad 56 - Ties of

Kinship - كتاب صِلَةِ الرَّحِم." *Sunnah.com*,

https://sunnah.com/adab:56.

al-Bukhari, Muhammad ibn Ismail. "Hadith on Anger: Truly strong

control themselves when enraged." *Faith in Allah*, 6 October

2010,

https://www.abuaminaelias.com/dailyhadithonline/2010/10/06/s

trong-control-anger/.

al-Bukhari, Muhammad ibn Ismail. "Hadith on Ansar: Love for

companions is part of faith." *Faith in Allah*, 2 May 2013,

https://www.abuaminaelias.com/dailyhadithonline/2013/05/02/l

ove-ansar-companions-faith/.

al-Bukhari, Muhammad ibn Ismail. "Hadith on Dua: The Prophet asks

Allah for light in his heart." *Faith in Allah*, 21 December 2020,

https://www.abuaminaelias.com/dailyhadithonline/2020/12/21/p

rophet-asks-nur-noor/.

al-Bukhari, Muhammad ibn Ismail. "Hadith on Faith: Not a believer when

he commits major sins." *Faith in Allah*, 26 March 2012,

https://www.abuaminaelias.com/dailyhadithonline/2012/03/26/i

man-commits-major-sins/.

al-Bukhari, Muhammad ibn Ismail. "Hadith on Fitrah: Five acts part of natural human instinct." *Faith in Allah*, 14 March 2014, https://www.abuaminaelias.com/dailyhadithonline/2014/03/14/fitrah-five-acts-nature/.

al-Bukhari, Muhammad ibn Ismail. "Hadith on Food: The Prophet's family rarely ate to their fill." *Faith in Allah*, 15 May 2011, https://www.abuaminaelias.com/dailyhadithonline/2011/05/15/ahl-al-bayt-eat-fill/.

al-Bukhari, Muhammad ibn Ismail. "Hadith on Ikhwah: Believer is a mirror to his brother." *Faith in Allah*, 13 October 2012, https://www.abuaminaelias.com/dailyhadithonline/2012/10/13/believer-mirror-to-brother/.

al-Bukhari, Muhammad ibn Ismail. "Hadith on Independence: Working for a living far better than begging." *Faith in Allah*, 9 October 2022, https://www.abuaminaelias.com/dailyhadithonline/2022/10/09/working-for-livelihood/.

al-Bukhari, Muhammad ibn Ismail. "Hadith on Sunnah: Trimming moustache, letting beard grow." *Faith in Allah*, 12 July 2012, https://www.abuaminaelias.com/dailyhadithonline/2012/07/12/trimming-moustache-let-beard-grow/.

al-Bukhari, Muhammad ibn Ismail. "Hadith on Sweets: The Prophet liked naturally sweet food." *Faith in Allah*, 13 July 2019,

https://www.abuaminaelias.com/dailyhadithonline/2019/07/13/p
rophet-liked-sweets-honey/.

al-Bukhari, Muhammad ibn Ismail. "Hadith on Women: Among greatest
trials for men is women." *Faith in Allah*, 23 October 2017,
https://www.abuaminaelias.com/dailyhadithonline/2017/10/23/g
reatest-fitnah-men-women/.

al-Bukhari, Muhammad ibn Ismail. "Sahih al-Bukhari 1135 - Prayer at
Night (Tahajjud) - كتاب التهجد." *Sunnah.com*,
https://sunnah.com/bukhari:1135.

al-Bukhari, Muhammad ibn Ismail. "Sahih al-Bukhari 2029 - Retiring to a
Mosque for Remembrance of Allah (I'tikaf) - كتاب الاعتكاف."
Sunnah.com, https://sunnah.com/bukhari:2029.

al-Bukhari, Muhammad ibn Ismail. "Sahih al-Bukhari 2576 - Gifts - كتاب
الهبة وفضلها والتحريض عليها." *Sunnah.com*,
https://sunnah.com/bukhari:2576.

al-Bukhari, Muhammad ibn Ismail. "Sahih al-Bukhari 2663 - Witnesses -
كتاب الشهادات." *Sunnah.com*, https://sunnah.com/bukhari:2663.

al-Bukhari, Muhammad ibn Ismail. "Sahih al-Bukhari 2707 -
Peacemaking - كتاب الصلح." *Sunnah.com*,
https://sunnah.com/bukhari:2707.

al-Bukhari, Muhammad ibn Ismail. "Sahih al-Bukhari 3154 - One-fifth of
Booty to the Cause of Allah (Khumus) - كتاب فرض الخمس."
Sunnah.com, https://sunnah.com/bukhari:3154.

al-Bukhari, Muhammad ibn Ismail. "Sahih al-Bukhari 3231 - Beginning
of Creation - كتاب بدء الخلق. " *Sunnah.com,*
https://sunnah.com/bukhari:3231.

al-Bukhari, Muhammad ibn Ismail. "Sahih al-Bukhari 3373 - Prophets -
كتاب أحاديث الأنبياء. " *Sunnah.com,*
https://sunnah.com/bukhari:3373.

al-Bukhari, Muhammad ibn Ismail. "Sahih al-Bukhari 3554 - Virtues and
Merits of the Prophet (pbuh) and his Companions - كتاب المناقب. "
Sunnah.com, https://sunnah.com/bukhari:3554.

al-Bukhari, Muhammad ibn Ismail. "Sahih al-Bukhari 3 - Revelation -
كتاب بدء الوحى. " *Sunnah.com,* https://sunnah.com/bukhari:3.

al-Bukhari, Muhammad ibn Ismail. "Sahih al-Bukhari 4101 - Military
Expeditions led by the Prophet (pbuh) (Al-Maghaazi) - كتاب
المغازى. " *Sunnah.com,* https://sunnah.com/bukhari:4101.

al-Bukhari, Muhammad ibn Ismail. "Sahih al-Bukhari 4418 - Military
Expeditions led by the Prophet (pbuh) (Al-Maghaazi) - كتاب
المغازى. " *Sunnah.com,* https://sunnah.com/bukhari:4418.

al-Bukhari, Muhammad ibn Ismail. "Sahih al-Bukhari 445 - Prayers
(Salat) - كتاب الصلاة. " *Sunnah.com,*
https://sunnah.com/bukhari:445.

al-Bukhari, Muhammad ibn Ismail. "Sahih al-Bukhari 5065 - Wedlock,
Marriage (Nikaah) - كتاب النكاح. " *Sunnah.com,*
https://sunnah.com/bukhari:5065.

al-Bukhari, Muhammad ibn Ismail. "Sahih al-Bukhari 5146 - Wedlock,
Marriage (Nikaah) - كتاب النكاح." *Sunnah.com*,
https://sunnah.com/bukhari:5146.

al-Bukhari, Muhammad ibn Ismail. "Sahih al-Bukhari 5199 - Wedlock,
Marriage (Nikaah) - كتاب النكاح." *Sunnah.com*,
https://sunnah.com/bukhari:5199.

al-Bukhari, Muhammad ibn Ismail. "Sahih al-Bukhari 5199 - Wedlock,
Marriage (Nikaah) - كتاب النكاح." *Sunnah.com*,
https://sunnah.com/bukhari:5199.

al-Bukhari, Muhammad ibn Ismail. "Sahih al-Bukhari 527 - Times of the
Prayers - كتاب مواقيت الصلاة." *Sunnah.com*,
https://sunnah.com/bukhari:527.

al-Bukhari, Muhammad ibn Ismail. "Sahih al-Bukhari 5394 - Food, Meals
- كتاب الأطعمة." *Sunnah.com*, https://sunnah.com/bukhari:5394.

al-Bukhari, Muhammad ibn Ismail. "Sahih al-Bukhari 5439 - Food, Meals
- كتاب الأطعمة." *Sunnah.com*, https://sunnah.com/bukhari:5439.

al-Bukhari, Muhammad ibn Ismail. "Sahih al-Bukhari 552 - Times of the
Prayers - كتاب مواقيت الصلاة." *Sunnah.com*,
https://sunnah.com/bukhari:552.

al-Bukhari, Muhammad ibn Ismail. "Sahih al-Bukhari 5767 - Medicine -
كتاب الطب." *Sunnah.com*, https://sunnah.com/bukhari:5767.

al-Bukhari, Muhammad ibn Ismail. "Sahih al-Bukhari 5768 - Medicine -
كتاب الطب." *Sunnah.com*, https://sunnah.com/bukhari:5768.

al-Bukhari, Muhammad ibn Ismail. "Sahih al-Bukhari 6464 - To make the Heart Tender (Ar-Riqaq) - كتاب الرقاق." *Sunnah.com*, https://sunnah.com/bukhari:6464.

al-Bukhari, Muhammad ibn Ismail. "Sahih al-Bukhari 6972 - Tricks - كتاب الحيل." *Sunnah.com*, https://sunnah.com/bukhari:6972.

al-Bukhari, Muhammad ibn Ismail. "Sahih al-Bukhari 7405 - Oneness, Uniqueness of Allah (Tawheed) - كتاب التوحيد." *Sunnah.com*, https://sunnah.com/bukhari:7405.

al-Bukhari, Muhammad ibn Ismail. "SAHIH BUKHARI, BOOK 65: Food, Meals." *IIUM*, https://www.iium.edu.my/deed/hadith/bukhari/065_sbt.html.

Al-Halawani, Ali. "5 Prophet's Hadiths About Smiling." *About Islam*, 29 June 2023, https://aboutislam.net/shariah/hadith/hadith-collections/5-hadiths-about-smiling/.

al-Isfahani, Abu Nu'aym Ahmad ibn 'Abdullah. "Shafi'i on Advice: Sincere advice is given in private, not public." *Faith in Allah*, 21 January 2018, https://www.abuaminaelias.com/dailyhadithonline/2018/01/21/shafiee-advice-private/.

al-Kafi, al-Jawab. "Ibn Abbas on Deeds: Good deeds bring light, evil deeds darkness." *Faith in Allah*, 2 April 2017, https://www.abuaminaelias.com/dailyhadithonline/2017/04/02/ibn-abbas-hasanat-nur/.

Al-Munajjid, Muhammed Salih. *Ruling on dyeing hair with black - Islam Question & Answer*, https://islamqa.info/en/answers/476/ruling-on-dyeing-hair-with-black.

Al-Munajjid, Muhammed Salih. *How to Control Anger in Islam - Islam Question & Answer*, https://islamqa.info/en/answers/658/how-to-control-anger-in-islam.

Al-Munajjid, Muhammed Salih. *How to Protect Yourself from the Evil Eye - Islam Question & Answer*, https://islamqa.info/en/answers/11359/how-to-protect-yourself-from-the-evil-eye.

Al-Munajjid, Muhammed Salih. "The Black Stone." *The Black Stone - Islam Question & Answer*, Islam Question & Answer, https://islamqa.info/en/answers/1902/the-black-stone.

Al-Munajjid, Muhammed Salih. "Eating habits and diet of the Prophet (peace and blessings of Allaah be upon him)." Islam Question & Answer, https://islamqa.info/en/answers/6503/eating-habits-and-diet-of-the-prophet-peace-and-blessings-of-allaah-be-upon-him.

al-Nawawi, Yahya ibn Sharaf. "Hadith 18, 40 Hadith an-Nawawi - Forty Hadith of an-Nawawi." *Sunnah.com*, https://sunnah.com/nawawi40:18.

al-Nawawi, Yahya ibn Sharaf. "Hadith 7, 40 Hadith an-Nawawi - Forty Hadith of an-Nawawi." *Sunnah.com*, https://sunnah.com/nawawi40:7.

al-Nawawi, Yahya ibn Sharaf. "Riyad as-Salihin 1079 - The Book of Virtues - كتاب الفضائل." *Sunnah.com*, https://sunnah.com/riyadussalihin:1079.

al-Nawawi, Yahya ibn Sharaf. "Riyad as-Salihin 1255 - The Book of Virtues - كتاب الفضائل." *Sunnah.com*, https://sunnah.com/riyadussalihin:1255.

al-Nawawi, Yahya ibn Sharaf. "Riyad as-Salihin 1526 - The Book of the Prohibited actions - كتاب الأمور المنهي عنها." *Sunnah.com*, https://sunnah.com/riyadussalihin:1526.

al-Naysaburi, Muslim ibn al-Hajjaj. "The Comprehensive Book - كتاب الجامع." *The Comprehensive Book - كتاب الجامع - Sunnah.com - Sayings and Teachings of Prophet Muhammad (صلى الله عليه و سلم)*, https://sunnah.com/urn/2117740.

al-Naysaburi, Muslim ibn al-Hajjaj. "Hadith - Marriage - Bulugh al-Maram." *Hadith - Marriage - Bulugh al-Maram - Sunnah.com - Sayings and Teachings of Prophet Muhammad (صلى الله عليه و سلم)*, https://sunnah.com/bulugh/8/101.

al-Naysaburi, Muslim ibn al-Hajjaj. "Hadith on Akhirah: Umar weeps at the poverty of the Prophet." *Faith in Allah*, 2 October 2019, https://www.abuaminaelias.com/dailyhadithonline/2019/10/02/u mar-weeps-for-prophet/.

al-Naysaburi, Muslim ibn al-Hajjaj. "Hadith on 'Ayn: Beware evil eye of envy, perform ghusl." *Faith in Allah*, 3 May 2014, https://www.abuaminaelias.com/dailyhadithonline/2014/05/03/a l-ayn-haqq-ghusl/.

al-Naysaburi, Muslim ibn al-Hajjaj. "Hadith on Faith: Allah loves strong believers more, but all are good." *Faith in Allah*, 20 April 2012, https://www.abuaminaelias.com/dailyhadithonline/2012/04/20/a llah-loves-strong-weak-believers/.

al-Naysaburi, Muslim ibn al-Hajjaj. "Hadith on Grudges: Not admitted into Paradise until they reconcile." *Faith in Allah*, 14 August 2012, https://www.abuaminaelias.com/dailyhadithonline/2012/08/14/n o-jannah-until-islah/.

al-Naysaburi, Muslim ibn al-Hajjaj. "Hadith on Leadership: The Muslim leader is a shield who defends them." *Faith in Allah*, 4 April 2012, https://www.abuaminaelias.com/dailyhadithonline/2012/04/04/h adith-on-leadership-the-leader-of-the-muslims-is-a-shield-who- defends-them-when-he-fears-allah/.

al-Naysaburi, Muslim ibn al-Hajjaj. "Sahih Muslim 1047a - The Book of
Zakat - كتاب الزكاة." *Sunnah.com*,
https://sunnah.com/muslim:1047a.

al-Naysaburi, Muslim ibn al-Hajjaj. "Sahih Muslim 2003a - The Book of
Drinks - كتاب الأشربة." *Sunnah.com*,
https://sunnah.com/muslim:2003a.

al-Naysaburi, Muslim ibn al-Hajjaj. "Sahih Muslim 2102b - The Book of
Clothes and Adornment - كتاب اللباس والزينة." *Sunnah.com*,
https://sunnah.com/muslim:2102b.

al-Naysaburi, Muslim ibn al-Hajjaj. "Sahih Muslim 2308a - The Book of
Virtues - كتاب الفضائل." *Sunnah.com*,
https://sunnah.com/muslim:2308a.

al-Naysaburi, Muslim ibn al-Hajjaj. "Sahih Muslim 2542b - The Book of
the Merits of the Companions - كتاب فضائل الصحابة رضى الله تعالى
عنهم." *Sunnah.com*, https://sunnah.com/muslim:2542b.

al-Naysaburi, Muslim ibn al-Hajjaj. "Sahih Muslim 2664 - The Book of
Destiny - كتاب القدر." *Sunnah.com*,
https://sunnah.com/muslim:2664.

al-Naysaburi, Muslim ibn al-Hajjaj. "Sahih Muslim 2822 - The Book of
Paradise, its Description, its Bounties and its Inhabitants - كتاب
الجنة وصفة نعيمها وأهلها." *Sunnah.com*,
https://sunnah.com/muslim:2822.

272

Al-Qaasim, Abd Al-Malik. *What Are the Conditions of Joking in Islam? -*
Islam Question & Answer,
https://islamqa.info/en/answers/22170/what-are-the-conditions-
of-joking-in-islam.

al-Qarni, A'id. *Muhammad as If You Can See Him.* International Islamic
Publishing House, 2008.

al-Qazwini, Abu Ja'far Muhammad ibn Yazid ibn Maja. "Hadith on
Beauty: Allah is beautiful and loves beauty." *Faith in Allah*, 21
May 2017,
https://www.abuaminaelias.com/dailyhadithonline/2017/05/21/a
llah-jamil-yuhibbu-jamal/.

al-Qazwini, Abu Ja'far Muhammad ibn Yazid ibn Maja. "Hadith on
Friendliness: Best people are kind, benefit others." *Faith in
Allah*, 11 February 2014,
https://www.abuaminaelias.com/dailyhadithonline/2014/02/11/b
eat-people-kind-friendly-beneficial/.

al-Qazwini, Abu Ja'far Muhammad ibn Yazid ibn Maja. "Hadith on
Gossip: Worst spread gossip, find faults, divide people." *Faith
in Allah*, 15 June 2019,
https://www.abuaminaelias.com/dailyhadithonline/2019/06/15/
worst-spread-gossip-find-faults/.

al-Qazwini, Abu Ja'far Muhammad ibn Yazid ibn Maja. "Sunan Ibn
Majah 224 - The Book of the Sunnah - كتاب المقدمة."
Sunnah.com, https://sunnah.com/ibnmajah:224.

al-Qazwini, Muhammad ibn Yazid ibn Majah. "Hadith on Deen: Islam is
characterized by its modesty." *Faith in Allah*, 14 June 2019,
https://www.abuaminaelias.com/dailyhadithonline/2019/06/14/k
huluq-islam-al-haya/.

al-Qazwini, Muhammad ibn Yazid ibn Majah. "Hadith on Habits: Best
deeds are consistent, even if small." *Faith in Allah*, 14
September 2015,
https://www.abuaminaelias.com/dailyhadithonline/2015/09/14/b
est-deeds-regular-small/.

al-Qazwini, Muhammad ibn Yazid ibn Majah. "Hadith on Jumu'ah:
Friday is an Eid, dress nice, wear perfume." *Faith in Allah*, 13
December 2013,
https://www.abuaminaelias.com/dailyhadithonline/2013/12/13/fr
iday-eid-dress-nice-perfume/.

al-Qazwini, Muhammad ibn Yazid ibn Majah. "Hadith on Trials: Prophets
rejoice at hardship, seeking reward." *Faith in Allah*, 23
February 2022,
https://www.abuaminaelias.com/dailyhadithonline/2022/02/23/p
rophets-rejoice-hardship/.

al-Qazwini, Muhammad ibn Yazid ibn Majah. "Sunan Ibn Majah 1197 -
Establishing the Prayer and the Sunnah Regarding Them -
كتاب إقامة الصلاة والسنة فيها." *Sunnah.com*,
https://sunnah.com/ibnmajah:1197.

al-Qazwini, Muhammad ibn Yazid ibn Majah. "Sunan Ibn Majah 3319 -
Chapters on Food - كتاب الأطعمة." *Sunnah.com*,
https://sunnah.com/ibnmajah:3319.

al-Qazwini, Muhammad ibn Yazid ibn Majah. "Sunan Ibn Majah 3319 -
Chapters on Food - كتاب الأطعمة." *Sunnah.com*,
https://sunnah.com/ibnmajah:3319.

al-Qazwini, Muhammad ibn Yazid ibn Majah. "Sunan Ibn Majah 3349 -
Chapters on Food - كتاب الأطعمة." *Sunnah.com*,
https://sunnah.com/ibnmajah:3349.

al-Qazwini, Muhammad ibn Yazid ibn Majah. "Sunan Ibn Majah 3662 -
Etiquette - كتاب الأدب." *Sunnah.com*,
https://sunnah.com/ibnmajah:3662.

al-Qazwini, Muhammad ibn Yazid ibn Majah. "Sunan Ibn Majah 3723 -
Etiquette - كتاب الأدب." *Sunnah.com*,
https://sunnah.com/ibnmajah:3723.

al-Qazwini, Muhammad ibn Yazid ibn Majah. "Sunan Ibn Majah 4217 -
Zuhd - كتاب الزهد." *Sunnah.com*,
https://sunnah.com/ibnmajah:4217.

al-Qazwini, Muhammad ibn Yazid ibn Majah. "Sunan Ibn Majah 4218 -

Zuhd - كتاب الزهد." *Sunnah.com*,

https://sunnah.com/ibnmajah:4218.

al-Qazwini, Muhammad ibn Yazid ibn Majah. "Sunan Ibn Majah 702 -

The Book of the Prayer - كتاب الصلاة." *Sunnah.com*,

https://sunnah.com/ibnmajah:702.

al-Quda'i, Musnad al-Shihab. "Hadith on Silence: Speak good and be

rewarded, be silent and safe." *Faith in Allah*, 10 March 2021,

https://www.abuaminaelias.com/dailyhadithonline/2021/03/10/s

peak-good-silent-safe/.

al-Qurtubi, Abu Abdullah Muhammad ibn Ahmad ibn Abi Bakr ibn Farh

al-Ansari al-Khazraji al-Andalusi. *Tafsir al-Qurtubi The General

Judgments of the Qur'an and Clarification of what it contains of

the Sunnah and Ayahs of Discrimination Juz 3: Surat al-

Baqarah 254 – Surah Ali Imran 95.* vol. 3, Diwan Press.

al-Tabarani, Abu al-Qasim Sulaiman ibn Ahmad ibn Ayub ibn

Muhammed ibn Makki ibn Khasafah an-Nisapuri al-Lakhmi.

"Hadith on Charity: Allah helps him as long as he helps others."

Faith in Allah, 14 September 2017,

https://www.abuaminaelias.com/dailyhadithonline/2017/09/14/s

adaqah-allah-help-others/

al-Tabari, Abu Ja'far Muhammad ibn Jarir. "Ibn Abbas on Patience:

Enemies become friends by forgiveness." *Faith in Allah*, 3

November 2021,

https://www.abuaminaelias.com/dailyhadithonline/2021/11/03/ibn-abbas-sabr-hilm/.

Al-Tabrizi, Muhammad ibn Abdullah Khatib. "Mishkat al-Masabih 3215 - Marriage - كتاب النكاح." *Sunnah.com*, https://sunnah.com/mishkat:3215.

Al-Tabrizi, Muhammad ibn Abdullah Khatib. "Mishkat al-Masabih 4180 - Foods - كتاب الأطعمة." *Sunnah.com*, https://sunnah.com/mishkat:4180.

Al-Tabrizi, Muhammad ibn Abdullah Khatib. "Mishkat al-Masabih 4180 - Foods - كتاب الأطعمة." *Sunnah.com*, https://sunnah.com/mishkat:4180.

an-Nasa'i, Ahmad ibn Shu'ayb ibn 'Ali. "Hadith on Independence: Allah's aid in self-sufficiency from begging." *Faith in Allah*, 9 October 2022, https://www.abuaminaelias.com/dailyhadithonline/2022/10/09/sufficiency-from-begging/.

an-Nasa'i, Ahmad ibn Shu'ayb ibn 'Ali. "Sunan an-Nasa'i 1905 - The Book of Funerals - كتاب الجنائز." *Sunnah.com*, https://sunnah.com/nasai:1905.

an-Nasa'i, Ahmad ibn Shu'ayb ibn 'Ali. "Sunan an-Nasa'i 2533 - The Book of Zakah - كتاب الزكاة." *Sunnah.com*, https://sunnah.com/nasai:2533.

an-Nasa'i, Ahmad ibn Shu'ayb ibn 'Ali. "Sunan an-Nasa'i 3057 - The
Book of Hajj - كتاب مناسك الحج." *Sunnah.com*,
https://sunnah.com/nasai:3057.

an-Nasa'i, Ahmad ibn Shu'ayb ibn 'Ali. "Sunan an-Nasa'i 6 - The Book of
Purification - كتاب الطهارة. *Sunnah.com*,
https://sunnah.com/nasai:6.

an-Nasa'i, Ahmad ibn Shu'ayb ibn 'Ali. "Sunan an-Nasa'i 831 - The Book
of Leading the Prayer (Al-Imamah) - كتاب الإمامة. *Sunnah.com*,
https://sunnah.com/nasai:831.

an-Nasa'i, Ahmad ibn Shu'ayb ibn 'Ali. "Sunan an-Nasa'i 831 - The Book
of Leading the Prayer (Al-Imamah) - كتاب الإمامة. *Sunnah.com*,
https://sunnah.com/nasai:831.

as-Sijistan, Abu Dawud Sulaiman ibn al-Ash'ath ibn Ishaq al-Azdi.
"Hadith on Salat: Prayers at night has great rewards." *Faith in
Allah*, 14 June 2016,
https://www.abuaminaelias.com/dailyhadithonline/2016/06/14/p
rayer-at-night/.

as-Sijistani, Abu Dawud Sulaiman ibn al-Ash'ath ibn Ishaq al-Azdi.
"Hadith on 'Ayn: Many Muslims die by the evil eye." *Faith in
Allah*, 20 April 2021,
https://www.abuaminaelias.com/dailyhadithonline/2021/04/20/d
eath-by-nazar/.

as-Sijistani, Abu Dawud Sulaiman ibn al-Ash'ath ibn Ishaq al-Azdi.

"Hadith on Backbiting: If Allah seeks his faults, he will be exposed." *Faith in Allah*, 4 December 2010, https://www.abuaminaelias.com/dailyhadithonline/2010/12/04/backbiting-faith-not-entered-hearts/.

as-Sijistani, Abu Dawud Sulaiman ibn al-Ash'ath ibn Ishaq al-Azdi.

"Hadith on Begging: Warning to self-sufficient beggars." *Faith in Allah*, 2 June 2020, https://www.abuaminaelias.com/dailyhadithonline/2020/06/02/warning-begging-jahannam/.

as-Sijistani, Abu Dawud Sulaiman ibn al-Ash'ath ibn Ishaq al-Azdi.

"Hadith on Tajdid: Righteous people will renew the religion." *Faith in Allah*, 9 September 2012, https://www.abuaminaelias.com/dailyhadithonline/2012/09/09/tajdid-deen-every-century/.

as-Sijistani, Abu Dawud Sulaiman ibn al-Ash'ath ibn Ishaq al-Azdi.

"Sunan Abi Dawud 1398 - Prayer (Kitab Al-Salat): Detailed Injunctions about Ramadan - كتاب شهر رمضان." *Sunnah.com*, https://sunnah.com/abudawud:1398.

as-Sijistani, Abu Dawud Sulaiman ibn al-Ash'ath ibn Ishaq al-Azdi.

"Sunan Abi Dawud 1748 - The Rites of Hajj (Kitab Al-Manasik Wa'l-Hajj) - كتاب المناسك." *Sunnah.com*, https://sunnah.com/abudawud:1748.

as-Sijistani, Abu Dawud Sulaiman ibn al-Ash'ath ibn Ishaq al-Azdi.

"Sunan Abi Dawud 2606 - Jihad (Kitab Al-Jihad) - كتاب الجهاد."
Sunnah.com, https://sunnah.com/abudawud:2606.

as-Sijistani, Abu Dawud Sulaiman ibn al-Ash'ath ibn Ishaq al-Azdi.

"Sunan Abi Dawud 2774 - Jihad (Kitab Al-Jihad) - كتاب الجهاد."
Sunnah.com, https://sunnah.com/abudawud:2774.

as-Sijistani, Abu Dawud Sulaiman ibn al-Ash'ath ibn Ishaq al-Azdi.

"Sunan Abi Dawud 3679 - Drinks (Kitab Al-Ashribah) - كتاب
الأشربة." Sunnah.com, https://sunnah.com/abudawud:3679.

as-Sijistani, Abu Dawud Sulaiman ibn al-Ash'ath ibn Ishaq al-Azdi.

"Sunan Abi Dawud 3767 - Foods (Kitab Al-At'imah) - كتاب
الأطعمة." Sunnah.com, https://sunnah.com/abudawud:3767.

as-Sijistani, Abu Dawud Sulaiman ibn al-Ash'ath ibn Ishaq al-Azdi.

"Sunan Abi Dawud 3836 - Foods (Kitab Al-At'imah) - كتاب
الأطعمة." Sunnah.com, https://sunnah.com/abudawud:3836.

as-Sijistani, Abu Dawud Sulaiman ibn al-Ash'ath ibn Ishaq al-Azdi.

"Sunan Abi Dawud 4078 - Clothing (Kitab Al-Libas) - كتاب اللباس."
Sunnah.com, https://sunnah.com/abudawud:4078.

as-Sijistani, Abu Dawud Sulaiman ibn al-Ash'ath ibn Ishaq al-Azdi.

"Sunan Abi Dawud 4163 - Combing the Hair (Kitab Al-Tarajjul)
- كتاب الترجل." Sunnah.com, https://sunnah.com/abudawud:4163.

as-Sijistani, Abu Dawud Sulaiman ibn al-Ash'ath ibn Ishaq al-Azdi.
"Sunan Abi Dawud 4833 - General Behavior (Kitab Al-Adab) -
كتاب الأدب." *Sunnah.com*, https://sunnah.com/abudawud:4833.

at-Tirmidhi, Abu 'Isa Muhammad ibn 'Isa. "Ash-Shama'il Al-
Muhammadiyah 122 - The Walking Of Rasoolullah - باب ما جاء
في مشية رسول الله صلى الله عليه وسلم." *Sunnah.com*,
https://sunnah.com/shamail:122.

at-Tirmidhi, Abu 'Isa Muhammad ibn 'Isa. "Ash-Shama'il Al-
Muhammadiyah 227 - The Laughing Of Rasoolullah - باب ما جاء
في ضحك رسول الله صلى الله عليه وسلم." *Sunnah.com*,
https://sunnah.com/shamail:227.

at-Tirmidhi, Abu 'Isa Muhammad ibn 'Isa. "Ash-Shama'il Al-
Muhammadiyah 329 - The Humbleness Of Sayyidina
Rasoolullah - باب ماجاء في تواضع رسول الله صلى الله عليه وسلم."
Sunnah.com, https://sunnah.com/shamail:329.

at-Tirmidhi, Abu 'Isa Muhammad ibn 'Isa. "Ash-Shama'il Al-
Muhammadiyah 330 - The Humbleness Of Sayyidina
Rasoolullah - باب ماجاء في تواضع رسول الله صلى الله عليه وسلم."
Sunnah.com, https://sunnah.com/shamail:330.

at-Tirmidhi, Abu 'Isa Muhammad ibn 'Isa. "Ash-Shama'il Al-
Muhammadiyah 332 - The Humbleness Of Sayyidina
Rasoolullah - باب ماجاء في تواضع رسول الله صلى الله عليه وسلم."
Sunnah.com, https://sunnah.com/shamail:332.

281

at-Tirmidhi, Abu 'Isa Muhammad ibn 'Isa. "Ash-Shama'il Al-Muhammadiyah 335 - The Humbleness Of Sayyidina Rasoolullah - باب ماجاء في تواضع رسول الله صلى الله عليه وسلم. *Sunnah.com*, https://sunnah.com/shamail:335.

at-Tirmidhi, Abu 'Isa Muhammad ibn 'Isa. "Ash-Shama'il Al-Muhammadiyah 34 - The Combing Of The Hair Of Rasoolullah - باب ما جاء في ترجل رسول الله صلى الله عليه وسلم. *Sunnah.com*, https://sunnah.com/shamail:34.

at-Tirmidhi, Abu 'Isa Muhammad ibn 'Isa. "Ash-Shama'il Al-Muhammadiyah 8 - The Noble Features Of Rasoolullah - باب ما جاء في خلق رسول الله صلى الله عليه وسلم. *Sunnah.com*, https://sunnah.com/shamail:8.

at-Tirmidhi, Abu 'Isa Muhammad ibn 'Isa. "Hadith on Dua: Allah angry when He is not asked." *Faith in Allah*, 28 May 2021, https://www.abuaminaelias.com/dailyhadithonline/2021/05/28/allah-angry-no-dua/.

at-Tirmidhi, Abu 'Isa Muhammad ibn 'Isa. "Hadith on Dua: Let one of you ask Allah for all of his needs." *Faith in Allah*, 28 March 2012, https://www.abuaminaelias.com/dailyhadithonline/2012/03/28/ask-allah-alone-for-needs/.

at-Tirmidhi, Abu 'Isa Muhammad ibn 'Isa. "Hadith on Dua: Nothing is nobler to Allah than supplication." *Faith in Allah*, 17 June 2014,

https://www.abuaminaelias.com/dailyhadithonline/2014/06/17/n
othing-nobler-dua/.

at-Tirmidhi, Abu 'Isa Muhammad ibn 'Isa. "Hadith on Elders: Gray hairs
in Islam are a blessing." *Faith in Allah*, 5 March 2013,
https://www.abuaminaelias.com/dailyhadithonline/2013/03/05/g
rey-hairs-in-islam/.

at-Tirmidhi, Abu 'Isa Muhammad ibn 'Isa. "Hadith on Family: Best of you
are best to their family." *Faith in Allah*, 28 May 2012,
https://www.abuaminaelias.com/dailyhadithonline/2012/05/28/b
est-of-you-best-family/.

at-Tirmidhi, Abu 'Isa Muhammad ibn 'Isa. "Hadith on Istighfar: Not a
persistent sinner if sincerely repenting." *Faith in Allah*, 26
December 2022,
https://www.abuaminaelias.com/dailyhadithonline/2022/12/26/s
tubborn-istighfar/.

at-Tirmidhi, Abu 'Isa Muhammad ibn 'Isa. "Hadith on Morning: Bless my
Ummah in their early mornings." *Faith in Allah*, 29 July 2013,
https://www.abuaminaelias.com/dailyhadithonline/2013/07/29/u
mmah-blessed-morning/.

at-Tirmidhi, Abu 'Isa Muhammad ibn 'Isa. "Hadith on Parents: Pleasure
of Allah in the pleasure of parents." *Faith in Allah*, 25 April
2013,

https://www.abuaminaelias.com/dailyhadithonline/2013/04/25/p
arents-pleasure-allah/.

at-Tirmidhi, Abu 'Isa Muhammad ibn 'Isa. "Hadith on Satiety: Those who
overeat are hungriest in Hereafter." *Faith in Allah*, 19 January
2021,
https://www.abuaminaelias.com/dailyhadithonline/2021/01/19/o
vereat-hungriest-akhirah/.

at-Tirmidhi, Abu 'Isa Muhammad ibn 'Isa. "Hadith on Sin: Black spot on
his heart until he repents." *Faith in Allah*, 13 September 2012,
https://www.abuaminaelias.com/dailyhadithonline/2012/09/13/b
lack-spot-heart-tawbah/.

at-Tirmidhi, Abu 'Isa Muhammad ibn 'Isa. "Jami` at-Tirmidhi 1943 -
Chapters on Righteousness And Maintaining Good Relations
With Relatives - كتاب البر والصلة عن رسول الله صلى الله عليه وسلم." ″
Sunnah.com, https://sunnah.com/tirmidhi:1943.

at-Tirmidhi, Abu 'Isa Muhammad ibn 'Isa. "Jami` at-Tirmidhi 1956 -
Chapters on Righteousness And Maintaining Good Relations
With Relatives - كتاب البر والصلة عن رسول الله صلى الله عليه وسلم." ″
Sunnah.com, https://sunnah.com/tirmidhi:1956.

at-Tirmidhi, Abu 'Isa Muhammad ibn 'Isa. "Jami` at-Tirmidhi 22 - The
Book on Purification - كتاب الطهارة عن رسول الله صلى الله عليه وسلم." ″
Sunnah.com, https://sunnah.com/tirmidhi:22.

at-Tirmidhi, Abu 'Isa Muhammad ibn 'Isa. "Jami` at-Tirmidhi 2315 - Chapters On Zuhd - كتاب الزهد عن رسول الله صلى الله عليه وسلم." Sunnah.com, https://sunnah.com/tirmidhi:2315.

at-Tirmidhi, Abu 'Isa Muhammad ibn 'Isa. "Jami` at-Tirmidhi 2501 - Chapters on the description of the Day of Judgement, Ar-Riqaq, and Al-Wara' - كتاب صفة القيامة والرقائق والورع عن رسول الله صلى الله." Sunnah.com, https://sunnah.com/tirmidhi:2501.

at-Tirmidhi, Abu 'Isa Muhammad ibn 'Isa. "Jami` at-Tirmidhi 2501 - Chapters on the description of the Day of Judgement, Ar-Riqaq, and Al-Wara' - كتاب صفة القيامة والرقائق والورع عن رسول الله صلى الله." Sunnah.com, https://sunnah.com/tirmidhi:2501.

at-Tirmidhi, Abu 'Isa Muhammad ibn 'Isa. "Jami` at-Tirmidhi 2797 - Chapters on Manners - كتاب الأدب عن رسول الله صلى الله عليه وسلم." Sunnah.com, https://sunnah.com/tirmidhi:2797.

at-Tirmidhi, Abu 'Isa Muhammad ibn 'Isa. "Jami` at-Tirmidhi 3371 - Chapters on Supplication - كتاب الدعوات عن رسول الله صلى الله عليه وسلم." Sunnah.com, https://sunnah.com/tirmidhi:3371.

at-Tirmidhi, Abu 'Isa Muhammad ibn 'Isa. "Jami` at-Tirmidhi 3373 - Chapters on Supplication - كتاب الدعوات عن رسول الله صلى الله عليه وسلم." Sunnah.com, https://sunnah.com/tirmidhi:3373.

at-Tirmidhi, Abu 'Isa Muhammad ibn 'Isa. "Jami` at-Tirmidhi 3635 - Chapters on Virtues - كتاب المناقب عن رسول الله صلى الله عليه وسلم." Sunnah.com, https://sunnah.com/tirmidhi:3635.

at-Tirmidhi, Abu 'Isa Muhammad ibn 'Isa. "Jami` at-Tirmidhi 3686 - Chapters on Virtues - كتاب المناقب عن رسول الله صلى الله عليه وسلم." *Sunnah.com*, https://sunnah.com/tirmidhi:3686.

at-Tirmidhi, Abu 'Isa Muhammad ibn 'Isa. "Jami` at-Tirmidhi 658 - The Book on Zakat - كتاب الزكاة عن رسول الله صلى الله عليه وسلم." *Sunnah.com*, https://sunnah.com/tirmidhi:658.

at-Tirmidhi, Abu 'Isa Muhammad ibn 'Isa. "Jami` at-Tirmidhi 745 - The Book on Fasting - كتاب الصوم عن رسول الله صلى الله عليه وسلم." *Sunnah.com*, https://sunnah.com/tirmidhi:745.

at-Tirmidhi, Abu 'Isa Muhammad ibn 'Isa. "Jami` at-Tirmidhi 747 - The Book on Fasting - كتاب الصوم عن رسول الله صلى الله عليه وسلم." *Sunnah.com*, https://sunnah.com/tirmidhi:747.

at-Tirmidhi, Muhammad ibn 'Isa. "Jami` at-Tirmidhi 3642 - Chapters on Virtues - كتاب المناقب عن رسول الله صلى الله عليه وسلم." *Sunnah.com*, https://sunnah.com/tirmidhi:3642.

Aultman. "World Smile Day - How Smiling Affects Your Brain." *Aultman Hospital*, 6 October 2017, https://aultman.org/blog/caring-for-you/world-smile-day-how-smiling-affects-your-brain/#/.

Azab, Marwa. "Why Sharing Your Goals Makes Them Less Achievable." *Psychology Today*, 1 January 2018, https://www.psychologytoday.com/us/blog/neuroscience-in-everyday-life/201801/why-sharing-your-goals-makes-them-less-achievable.

Bleske, April L., and David M. Buss. "Can men and women be just friends?" *UT Psychology Labs*, https://labs.la.utexas.edu/buss/files/2015/09/just_friends_2000.pdf.

Brooten, Michelle C. "Excessive Talking: Causes, Types, Social Strategies." *Verywell Health*, 28 June 2023, https://www.verywellhealth.com/excessive-talking-5224128.

Brown, Marishka. "Get Enough Sleep - MyHealthfinder | health.gov." *Office of Disease Prevention and Health Promotion*, 1 August 2021, https://health.gov/myhealthfinder/healthy-living/mental-health-and-relationships/get-enough-sleep.

Cascio, Christopher N., et al. "Self-affirmation activates brain systems associated with self-related processing and reward and is reinforced by future orientation." 2016, pp. 621-629. *National Library of Medicine*, doi: 10.1093/scan/nsv136.

Castine, Michael. "Can Being Scared Be Good for Your Health? | Ochsner Health." *Ochsner Blog*, 27 October 2016, https://blog.ochsner.org/articles/can-being-scared-be-good-for-your-health.

Chaurasia, Akhilanand, et al. "Miswak in oral cavity - An update." 2013, pp. 98-101. *National Library of Medicine*, doi: 10.1016/j.jobcr.2012.09.004.

Daily Stoic. "Justice: The Most Important Virtue." *Daily Stoic*, 5 March

2020, https://dailystoic.com/justice-the-most-important-virtue/.

Dawood, Abu. *What Are the Conditions of Joking in Islam? - Islam*

Question & Answer,

https://islamqa.info/en/answers/22170/what-are-the-conditions-

of-joking-in-islam.

Doufesh, Hazem, et al. "Effect of Muslim prayer (Salat) on a

electroencephalography and its relationship with autonomic

nervous system activity." July, pp. 558-562. *National Library of*

Medicine, doi: 10.1089/acm.2013.0426.

Elias, Abu Amina. "Cleanliness and pleasant appearance in Islam."

Faith in Allah, 22 January 2018,

https://www.abuaminaelias.com/cleanliness-and-pleasant-

appearance-in-islam/.

Elias, Abu Amina. "True men, manhood, and masculinity in Islam." *Faith*

in Allah, 28 March 2018, https://www.abuaminaelias.com/true-

men-manhood-and-masculinity-in-islam/.

Faris, Mohammed. "Know your Past - ProductiveMuslim.com."

Productive Muslim, 14 September 2011,

https://productivemuslim.com/know-your-past/.

Fuhrel, Andrea. "Selfless volunteering might lengthen your life, research

suggests." *American Psychological Association*, 1 November

2011, https://www.apa.org/monitor/2011/11/volunteering.

Gallo, Amy. "How to Give an Employee Feedback About Their

  Appearance." *Harvard Business Review*, 26 May 2017,

  https://hbr.org/2017/05/how-to-give-an-employee-feedback-

  about-their-appearance.

Gordon, Sherri. "Understanding the Impact of Rumors and Gossip."

  Verywell Family, 18 July 2020,

  https://www.verywellfamily.com/understanding-the-impact-of-

  rumors-and-gossip-460625.

Hanbal, Ahmad ibn. "Islam is against racism and prejudice." *Faith in*

  Allah, 25 July 2013, https://www.abuaminaelias.com/islam-

  against-racism-bigotry/.

Hanbal, Ahmad ibn. "Musnad Ahmad 190 - Musnad ʿUmar b. al-Khattab

  (ra) - .مُسْنَدِ عُمَرَ بْنِ الْخَطَّابِ رَضِيَ اللَّهُ عَنْهُ." *Sunnah.com*,

  https://sunnah.com/ahmad:190.

Hilbrand, Sonja. "Caregiving within and beyond the family is associated

  with lower mortality for the caregiver: A prospective study."

  Evolution and Human Behavior, vol. 38, no. 3, 2017, pp. 397-

  403. *Science Direct*,

  https://doi.org/10.1016/j.evolhumbehav.2016.11.010.

Howkins, Michael. "The Art of Silence: How Speaking Less Can Make

  You More Intelligent, Compassionate, and Successful."

  Medium, 24 February 2020, https://medium.com/the-ascent/the-art-of-silence-how-speaking-less-can-make-you-more-intelligent-compassionate-and-successful-ff13b7f7afc4.

ibn Hanbal, Ahmad. "Hadith on Begging: Prohibition of persistently asking without need." *Faith in Allah*, 9 October 2022, https://www.abuaminaelias.com/dailyhadithonline/2022/10/09/persistently-asking/.

ibn Hanbal, Ahmad. "Hadith on Independence: The Prophet orders Abu Bakr not to ask people." *Faith in Allah*, 6 December 2020, https://www.abuaminaelias.com/dailyhadithonline/2020/12/06/prophet-orders-not-to-ask/.

ibn Hanbal, Ahmad. "Hadith on Leadership: Intense regret of sinful leaders on Judgment Day." *Faith in Allah*, 18 June 2022, https://www.abuaminaelias.com/dailyhadithonline/2022/06/18/intense-regret-leaders/.

ibn Hanbal, Ahmad. "Hadith on Milk: Blessing in pure organic grassfed cow's milk." *Faith in Allah*, 21 January 2018, https://www.abuaminaelias.com/dailyhadithonline/2018/01/21/barakah-grassfed-baqarah-milk/.

ibn Hanbal, Ahmad. "Hadith on Mockery: Man sinks into Hell because of bad joke." *Faith in Allah*, 22 May 2020, https://www.abuaminaelias.com/dailyhadithonline/2020/05/22/sinks-into-hell-bad-joke/.

ibn Hanbal, Ahmad. "Hadith on Zina: Would you like that for your

    mother, sister?" *Faith in Allah*, 9 May 2014,

    https://www.abuaminaelias.com/dailyhadithonline/2014/05/09/z

    ina-adulter-like-sister/.

ibn Hanbal, Ahmad. "Musnad Ahmad 190 - Musnad `Umar b. al-Khattab

    (ra). - مُسْنَدِ عُمَرَ بْنِ الْخَطَّابِ رَضِيَ اللَّهُ عَنْهُ." *Sunnah.com*,

    https://sunnah.com/ahmad:190.

ibn Hanbal, Ahmad. "Musnad Ahmad 266, 267 - Musnad `Umar b. al-

    Khattab (ra). - مُسْنَدِ عُمَرَ بْنِ الْخَطَّابِ رَضِيَ اللَّهُ عَنْهُ." *Sunnah.com*,

    https://sunnah.com/ahmad:266.

Iliades, Chris, and Pat F. Bass. "The Truth About Lies and Longevity -

    Longevity Center." *Everyday Health*, 14 July 2010,

    https://www.everydayhealth.com/longevity/truth-about-lies-and-

    longevity.aspx.

Iliades, Chris, and Pat F. Bass. "The Truth About Lies and Longevity -

    Longevity Center." *Everyday Health*, 14 July 2010,

    https://www.everydayhealth.com/longevity/truth-about-lies-and-

    longevity.aspx.

Islam Q&A. *Dealing with the fitnah (temptation) of women - Islam*

    Question & Answer,

    https://islamqa.info/en/answers/33651/dealing-with-the-fitnah-

    temptation-of-women.

Islam Q&A. *Fasting on Mondays and Thursdays or on Three Days of each Month? - Islam Question & Answer*, https://islamqa.info/en/answers/69781/fasting-on-mondays-and-thursdays-or-on-three-days-of-each-month.

Islam Q&A. *Did the Prophet (blessings and peace of Allah be upon him) and his Companions (may Allah be pleased with them) do any kind of athletic training or exercise? - Islam Question & Answer*, https://islamqa.info/en/answers/225943/did-the-prophet-blessings-and-peace-of-allah-be-upon-him-and-his-companions-may-allah-be-pleased-with-them-do-any-kind-of-athletic-training-or-exercise.

Islam Q&A. *Can You Pluck Grey Hair? - Islam Question & Answer*, https://islamqa.info/en/answers/171195/it-is-makrooh-to-pluck-grey-hair-from-the-head-and-moustache.

Islam Q&A. *The virtue of one who regularly offers the five daily prayers and does them as enjoined - Islam Question & Answer*, 7 6 2018, https://islamqa.info/en/answers/238527/the-virtue-of-one-who-regularly-offers-the-five-daily-prayers-and-does-them-as-enjoined.

Islam Q&A. *The virtue of staying in the mosque after Fajr prayer - Islam Question & Answer*, https://islamqa.info/en/answers/100009/the-virtue-of-staying-in-the-mosque-after-fajr-prayer.

Islam Q&A. *Du'a Between Adhan and Iqamah: Recommended? - Islam Question & Answer*, https://islamqa.info/en/answers/5666/dua-between-adhan-and-iqamah-recommended.

Islam Q&A. *When to Say Allahumma Barik - Islam Question & Answer*, https://islamqa.info/en/answers/335259/when-to-say-allahumma-barik.

Jangda, Abdul Nasir. "Story of Prophet Muhammad and a Wrestling Champ." *About Islam*, 3 January 2020, https://aboutislam.net/reading-islam/about-muhammad/story-prophet-muhammad-wrestling-champ/.

Khan, Ashley Pearson. "7 Quran Verses & Hadith about Parents." *Muslimi*, 5 August 2022, https://muslimi.com/7-quran-verses-hadith-about-parents/.

Khan, Muhammad Muhsin. *Sahih Al-Bukhari: Concise Version*. Kazi Publications, Incorporated, 1994.

Kim, Jean. "The Psychology of Neighbors." *Psychology Today*, 8 June 2020, https://www.psychologytoday.com/us/blog/culture-shrink/202006/the-psychology-neighbors.

Lowndes, Leil. *How to talk to anyone*. McGraw-Hill Education, 2003.

Mahmoud, Majed. *Lessons from the Prophet ﷺ on The Art of Influence*. Al-Maghrib Institute.

Mohammed, Azhaan. *Character of Muhammad: Peace Be Upon Him*. 2022.

Motala, Suhail. "A Sahabi (radiyallahu 'anhu) who requested permission to commit zina – Hadith Answers." *Hadith Answers*, 19 June 2020, https://hadithanswers.com/a-sahabi-radiyallahu-anhu-who-requested-permission-to-commit-zina/.

Mubārakfūrī, Ṣafī al-Raḥmān. *The Sealed Nectar: Biography of the Noble Prophet*. Darussalam, 2002.

Navarro, Joe, and Marvin Karlins. *What every BODY is saying*. HarperCollins, 2008.

Nilsson, Erik. "Overweight and cognition." *Scandinavian Journal of Psychology*, vol. 50, no. 6, 2009, pp. 660-667, doi.org/10.1111/j.1467-9450.2009.00777.x.

Novotney, Amy. "What happens in your brain when you give a gift?" *American Psychological Association*, 9 December 2022, https://www.apa.org/topics/mental-health/brain-gift-giving.

Paul, Margaret. "Over-Talking: The Need to Talk Too Much." *Inner Bonding*, 9 June 2014, https://www.innerbonding.com/show-article/3793/over-talking-the-need-to-talk-too-much.html.

"Physically Strengthen based on Sunnah — Learn Islam." https://learn-islam.org/strengthen-based-on-sunnah.

Pigliucci, Massimo. "Stoicism." *Internet Encyclopedia of Philosophy*, https://iep.utm.edu/stoicism/.

Richter, Amy. "Top 6 Foods That Can Cause Acne." *Healthline*, 24 January 2018, https://www.healthline.com/nutrition/foods-that-cause-acne.

Sallabi, 'Ali Muhammad. *Abu Bakr As-Siddeeq His Life & Times*. International Islamic Publishing House, 2012.

Sallabi, 'Ali Muhammad Muhammad. *'Umar Ibn Al-Khaṭṭâb: His Life and Times*. vol. 2, International Islamic Publishing House, 2007.

Schulz, Jodi. *Using a person's name in conversation - MSU Extension*, 12 January 2017, https://www.canr.msu.edu/news/using_a_persons_name_in_conversation.

Seitz, Adrienne. "Overeating Effects: 6 Health Impacts and How to Stop." *Greatist*, 3 February 2021, https://greatist.com/health/overeating-effects.

Seitz, Adrienne. "Overeating Effects: 6 Health Impacts and How to Stop." *Greatist*, 3 February 2021, https://greatist.com/health/overeating-effects#6-effects-of-overeating.

Shah, Sejal. "Morning Meditation: How to Breathe and Meditate As You Start Each Day." *ArtofLiving.org*, 12 July 2020, https://www.artofliving.org/us-en/tips-for-morning-meditation-to-help-you-reap-the-benefits-all-day-long.

SoP. "Consistency Theory." *The Science of Psychotherapy*, 4
September 2013,
https://www.thescienceofpsychotherapy.com/consistency-
theory/.

Sorensen, Michael S. "Validation: The Most Powerful Relationship Skill
You Were Never Taught." *Michael S. Sorensen*,
https://michaelssorensen.com/validation-the-most-powerful-
relationship-skill-you-were-never-taught/.

Stephens, William O. "Stoic Ethics." *Internet Encyclopedia of
Philosophy*, https://iep.utm.edu/stoiceth/.

Stibich, Mark. "10 Big Benefits of Smiling." *Verywell Mind*, 17 February
2023, https://www.verywellmind.com/top-reasons-to-smile-
every-day-2223755.

Vadlamani, Sonia. "8 manifestation techniques: understanding the law
of attraction." *Happiness.com*, 11 October 2020,
https://www.happiness.com/magazine/personal-
growth/manifestation-techniques-the-law-of-attraction/.

Wade, Danielle. "Can You Use Humor as a Coping Mechanism?" *Psych
Central*, 28 June 2022, https://psychcentral.com/lib/humor-as-
weapon-shield-and-psychological-salve.

Walid, Dawud. *Futuwwah And Raising Males Into Sacred Manhood*.
Imam Ghazali Institute.

Waliullah, Shah. "Hadith 34, 40 Hadith Shah Waliullah - Forty Hadith of

    Shah Waliullah Dehlawi." *Sunnah.com*,

    https://sunnah.com/shahwaliullah40:34.

Weaver, Tobias. "What Are The 4 Stoic Virtues?" *Orion Philosophy*, 17

    October 2019, https://www.orionphilosophy.com/stoic-blog/4-

    stoic-virtues.

Weir, Kirsten. "Forgiveness can improve mental and physical health."

    American Psychological Association, 1 January 2017,

    https://www.apa.org/monitor/2017/01/ce-corner.

Wolny, Nick. "Why you love setting goals more than pursuing them,

    according to science." *Fast Company*, 4 August 2021,

    https://www.fastcompany.com/90662001/why-you-love-setting-

    goals-more-than-pursuing-them-according-to-science.

Worthington, Everett L. "The New Science of Forgiveness | Greater

    Good." *Greater Good Science Center*, 1 September 2004,

    https://greatergood.berkeley.edu/article/item/the_new_science

    _of_forgiveness.

Younkin, Lainey. "What Happens to Your Body When You Eat Too

    Much." *EatingWell*, 6 May 2021,

    https://www.eatingwell.com/article/7900720/what-happens-to-

    your-body-when-you-eat-too-much/.

Zahra, Umm Fatima. "Muslima Sunnah Beauty Guide." *Muslima Guide*,
23 August 2020, https://muslimaguide.com/muslima-sunnah-
beauty-guide/.

Zahra, Umm Fatima. "The Natural Beauty of Noor." *Muslima Guide*, 9
October 2019, https://muslimaguide.com/the-natural-beauty-of-
noor/.

Zakrzewski, Vicki. "How Humility Will Make You the Greatest Person
Ever." *Greater Good Science Center*, 12 January 2016,
https://greatergood.berkeley.edu/article/item/humility_will_mak
e_you_greatest_person_ever.